The *Custom* HARLEY

The *Custom* HARLEY

JOHN CARROLL

Photographs by
GARRY STUART

Foreword by **ARLEN NESS**

SMITHMARK

A Salamander Book

This edition published in 1995 by SMITHMARK Publishers Inc.
16 East 32nd Street, New York, NY 10016

1 3 5 7 9 8 6 4 2

SMITHMARK books are available for bulk purchase for sales
promotion and premium use. For details write or call the manager
of special sales, SMITHMARK Publishers Inc. 16 East 32nd Street,
New York, NY 10016; (212) 532-6600

ISBN 0 8317 5512 1

All correspondence concerning the content of this
book should be addressed to
Salamander Books Ltd,
129–137 York Way, London N7 9LG, England

Credits
Editor: Richard Collins
Designer: John Heritage
Photographer: Garry Stuart
Filmset by Flair plan Photo-typesetting Ltd
Color reproduction P & W Graphics, Singapore
Printed in Italy

Additional captions
1 Hamsters MC detail on a Harley speedo.
2 A trio of riders on customized Evos.
4 Clive Maye's custom rigid Panhead.
6 The Evolution engine in Nigel Saxon's custom bike.
8 An Evo with a custom, urban grafitti paint scheme.
10 The Xzotic Eye, a bike built by Lawayne Matthies.
Endpapers A Softail chopper built by Arlen Ness.

CONTENTS

FOREWORD BY ARLEN NESS

I GOT MY FIRST HARLEY in 1966. I had no idea then that that bike would change my life so completely. I never set out to be any kind of celebrity. All I wanted was to have one of the coolest bikes in town.

That word 'cool' has sure had a lot of definitions over the years. Long forks, sportster tanks and raked frames have come and gone. Custom paint has gone from murals, to graphics, to monochrome jobs. Bikes have gotten tall, gotten low, gotten stretched, gotten bobbed. The only thing that remains constant is the fact that we just can't seem to leave them alone. Why not? In my case, I would have to say that I like things to be a little more personalized than they come from the factory. I like to change things. Many times, a stock bike just doesn't look right. Maybe the wheel doesn't sit over the fender right, or the handlebars are ugly, or it sits too high off the ground, or … you get the picture.

It's a question of vision. A successful custom bike builder can **see** how a bike will look finished before he ever begins. He can conceive how the lines of the bike will flow and create a unified image, and also reflect the current (or upcoming) trends in custom bikes. This conceptual process is really the hardest part of the whole thing. You have to know what you're building, or how will you know when you're done? I have been lucky enough to be blessed with this sort of vision, and to be able to associate with many talented people to help me achieve these visions.

These last few years have seen such a dramatic increase in interest in custom motorcycles, it's hard to believe we used to do this just for fun. I have watched my company go from a three-man operation ten years ago to employing over thirty people. We have had to keep moving to bigger and bigger locations as we've grown, to the point where, as I write, we are now preparing to build a brand new facility to house our operation.

Where is the custom bike scene going? I've noticed an increasing sophistication in the custom bike owner. When I started doing this, you couldn't buy **anything** to customize a bike. You had to adapt things off of other bikes, or make them from scratch. For better or worse, the custom builder today has things much easier. Parts availability for the custom builder has never been as great as it is now, and companies like mine are constantly expanding the possibilities. Custom bikes are getting very high tech, and we anticipate that the demand for our style of parts will only grow.

The American motorcycle aftermarket has grown to such an extent that it is possible now to build an American V-Twin custom bike completely from aftermarket parts, without using **any** parts from Milwaukee, and, since the quality of the aftermarket manufacturers generally has improved a great deal, that bike is as roadworthy as one from the factory. In our case, I feel our smaller production runs allow us to be far more innovative in our designs, and at the same time keep a tighter reign on quality.

The future of the custom bike has never looked brighter. The many new bike owners, for the most part, have more money to devote to their machines than in the old days. It may sound slightly mercenary, but it sure does make it easier to produce expensive parts if there is someone out there to buy them. Also, many very talented people are being attracted to custom bike building because of the money that has become available. An infusion of talent like that cannot help but improve the field.

I feel we are entering a new golden age of American motorcycles. With as many talented people involved in custom bike building as there are today, what lies in the future is far more exciting than anything that has happened yet! As you will see in the pages to come, the sky is the limit for the custom bike. I hope you enjoy it.

Arlen Ness

Arlen Ness
San Leandro, California

INTRODUCTION

TEN THOUSAND or more black biker T-shirts proclaim their wearers' allegiance to Harley–Davidson with the slogan, 'If I had to explain you wouldn't understand'. Like so many clichés there is a ring of truth to it. This might appear to negate the need for an introduction to a book on the very subject but its purpose is to set the scene rather than explain.

As with so many aspects of life in the second half of the twentieth century, motorcycling on both sides of the Atlantic was affected by World War Two and this theme crops up throughout this book. In America the returning GIs flooded into motorcycling using Uncle Sam's dollars to buy a Harley or an Indian. Some guys came home and wanted things to get back to 'normal' but for others it wasn't so easy and they were looking for more action. It was to be found in the saddle of a big motorcycle. Many rural American towns saw their first tourists arrive in the shape of city boys on motorcycles who were more interested in the tavern and the local girls. The prevailing social conditions of the time and the problems of the returning servicemen have been well documented by the likes of James Jones and Bill Mauldin. Those early days seemed to reach a pinnacle in terms of notoriety in July 1947 at the AMA races at Hollister in northern California. At the event things got somewhat out of control: a few riders were hospitalized, a few were jailed and most of them rode home after the weekend. The American Motorcyclist Association made the statement that only 1 per cent of riders behaved in such a fashion. The label stuck and outlaw clubs still sport a One Percenter patch today.

It is possible that nothing would ever have come of custom biking beyond being a niche within the whole thriving motorcycle scene as it was then, with a small percentage of riders aboard flat track-style Bobbers, except for the fact that Stanley Kramer read the reports of the incident in **Life** magazine. He made a film with a fictionalized screenplay of the incident that starred Lee Marvin and Marlon Brando. It hit the cinemas in 1954 and inspired young, white, working class kids from the cities to emulate the 'heroes' from **The Wild One** – especially the style of bearded Lee Marvin in a sleeveless jacket on a chopped Hog. Irrevocably the link between modified motorcycles and trouble had been made and, as is so often the case, the media as a form of communication fanned the flames. This may seem somewhat removed from the core subject of a book dedicated to custom Harleys but there is however a direct connection. Several decades after that particular film was made motorcycles and motorcycling apparel is being sold using words like 'individual', 'freedom', 'rugged' and even 'rebellious'. Riders are said to be 'living life their way', they are claimed to be the 'last frontiersmen' and the last in a line that stretches back through cowboys and pirates to Vikings and Celts. The reality is that the image, and the trade, is based on a sanitized version of the wild and lawless image, the seeds of which were sown on that 4 July in Hollister, and harvested on celluloid. Harley–Davidson themselves have used a clip from the film in their official video that has been released worldwide.

The sixties saw the chopper inexorably linked with the outlaw motorcycle clubs, especially in the eyes of the newspapers and film makers. Newspapers seemed to delight in lurid reporting of the salacious goings-on involving motorcyclists. For once it was the same in Europe – Britain at least, where motorcycle borne 'rockers' clashed with scooter-mounted 'mods' at English holiday resorts. A series of films that continued to portray chopper riders as hoodlums were made, including Roger Corman's **Wild Angels** of 1966. Three years later though, another film arrived that placed chopper riders firmly beyond the pale of normal society: **Easyrider**. Released in 1969 it redefined the chopper rider as dope smoking hippy, coming as it did during the uncertainties of the Vietnam War and highlighting the conflict between the redneck culture and that of the emerging 'longhairs'. The custom bike scene on both sides of the Atlantic would for a while, at least, co-exist alongside the hippy culture. Ultimately though the bike culture would be the only one that would survive without metamorphosizing into something else.

Unlike **The Wild One** (which was banned in Britain until 1968) **Easyrider** was screened worldwide and had an immediate effect. In the same way as **The Wild One** it tried to show the shocking truth about a minority within motorcycling and succeeded in spawning thousands of imitators. It is hard to overestimate just how powerful the influence of each of these films was. There were others such as the dramatic **Electra-Glide in Blue** and the nostalgic and nihilistic **The Loveless** of the early seventies and eighties respectively, but neither had the impact of the earlier movies. Films such as **Any Which Way But Loose** simply portrayed bikers on custom bikes in the role of circus clowns and beyond that the motorcycle was on the whole relegated to a supporting role, with

the possible exceptions of **Mask**, which starred Cher, and **Stone**, which was made in Australia. Alongside the movie business there was an industry that generated pulp fiction stories that dwelt on the real and imagined doings of certain motorcycle clubs.

Maybe it is true that there ain't no such thing as bad publicity because, despite such adverse reporting, custom bike building flourished; as chapters in this book show, many of the famous names in American custom bike building worked right through this period. The actual motorcycles themselves have been ever changing and ever evolving. There are several reasons for this; for example, custom bike builders have been quick to take advantage of new technology as it becomes available. In the fifty years since World War Two the materials used in motorcycle construction have undergone nothing short of revolutionary change so it is inevitable that styles will have progressed. Similarly metalworking techniques have also progressed; the advent of Mig and Tig welding means that certain jobs can be carried out to a higher standard while

Below: The chopper gives the rider an upright, disdainful view of the world from behind apehanger handlebars (left). Flathead Phil's bike (below) is an early chopper based around Harley's venerable 45cu. in. flathead. Phil has styled himself on Willem Dafoe's role in **The Loveless**.

other jobs become possible, such as heavily modifying gas tanks with a welder. Thirdly, custom motorcycle building is a competitive business; new customs are unveiled at big shows and the best take home the trophies. However, the winner cannot rest on his laurels because the losers will be working on a new creation. Certain shows such as The Oakland Roadster Show and The Rat's Hole Custom Show at Daytona and more recently at Sturgis have become institutions, while other shows around the world have followed. In England, for example, the Kent Chapter of the Hells Angels MC organize the annual Kent Custom Bike Show. One of the rules is that all entered bikes have to be ridden to be eligible for any of the trophies. The longstanding annual event attracts bikes and bikers from all over Europe. One aspect of the factory sponsored Harley Owners' Group events is that at events there will be a ride-in custom show. In fact the importance of riding Harleys and entering custom shows has partially eclipsed the competitive origins of events at Daytona, Sturgis and Laconia which were started around races, hillclimbs and gypsy tours.

Because of the ever changing nature of custom biking there is no constant reference beyond the annual aftermarket catalogues and the monthly magazines, of which **Easyriders** is undoubtedly the most famous. There have been a number of others and there is a range of newcomers about at present. Old issues of **Easyriders** are custom biking's equivalent of the Dead Sea Scrolls. The magazine is decades old and charts the changing styles of choppers, whether it was the trend toward shorter front ends after the excesses of the seventies, or toward gold plating, the decline of the cissy bar and Maltese cross mirrors. It also chronicled in its own inimitable way the introduction of the Evolution engine, the return of apehangers, the formation of the Harley Owners' Group and every other shift within the custom bike world.

To bring the whole scenario up to date, recent years have seen a shift toward respectability because professional people also want a piece of the action. They have flooded into Harley riding in unprecedented numbers, bringing a flood of dollars to both dealers and custom builders doors. The Harley–Davidson factory is steadily increasing production to meet a still growing demand; in the twelve months to December 1994 Harley shipped 95,811 motorcycles, a growth of 17 percent over the previous year. Of this figure 20 percent, a total of 29,313 Harley–Davidsons, were exported from the USA; such is the worldwide demand. Export markets include Europe, Australasia and Japan. To some the newcomers are seen as unwelcome intruders and are derisorily referred to as RUBs – Rich Urban Bikers – but they don't seem to care. They are too busy enjoying themselves riding their bikes – just like the original hardcore riders did – which is, when all is said and done, what it is all about.

Left: Wide handlebars and a big Harley on a country backroad. The forward mounted footpegs and the low seat height allow the rider to sit relaxed and upright – just easyriding. This differentiates the chopper rider from the sportsbike rider who adopts a forward leaning position.

The formation of the Harley Owners' Group (HOG) was seen by some as an attempt by Harley–Davidson to reclaim motorcycling's family traditions from the one percenters. The traditions they sought to reclaim were those of the forties and fifties when Harley (and Indian) ownership revolved around dealer-sponsored events and competitions such as Hare and Hounds, Gypsy Tours and picnics. This was in some ways something of a contradiction because the styles of officially licenced leather jackets – and indeed of factory choppers – were based on the styles that had been made famous by the 'rebels'. Others saw the whole thing through more cynical eyes and considered it to be little more than a massive marketing exercise. Either way, the contradiction exists – Harley want their bikes to be ridden by 'nice' people but rely on their rebellious image to sell the bikes to those people. Nowhere is this dichotomy more pronounced than in the fact that both The Law and the outlaw ride Harleys. Now, maybe there's a bit of the cowboy in both sides; after all, the James Gang rode horses as did the various law enforcement

Above: It's hard to overestimate the impact of the film **Easyrider**. This chopper was built twenty-five years after the film was made but is based around the same frame and has similar lines overall, albeit with some modern touches. Roll 'em boys …

officials who pursued them. The difference is in the way they did it, and so it is with both motorcycle cops and those on choppers. The motorcycle cop wears a uniform that includes a leather jacket, motorcycle boots and shades; so does the outlaw. The motorcycle cop rides a Harley that is customized in a specific way; so does the outlaw. The difference is simply that one group are seen as the guardians of law and order while the others are seen to be in defiance of it. Harley are no doubt aware of this and see a potential problem if such attitudes are perpetuated. One of the things they have done in an attempt to alleviate the situation is to market official Harley–Davidson T-shirts that read, 'Good Guys wear Black'. And so they do.

ORIGINS AND INFLUENCES

CUSTOM BIKE BUILDING has been continually evolving for more than fifty years. It started in the last years before World War II but really took off immediately after the war as thousands of former GIs flooded into motorcycling. Back then customizing, or 'bobbing' as it was known, meant modifying your Harley or Indian yourself. The tools used were the rider's own or those of a buddy and the parts were from other motorcycles or home-made. 'Bobbers' had all the surplus parts chopped off and so the term 'chopper' was born. The debut of the K-model Sportster in 1953 meant that smaller, lighter parts, such as the now ubiquitous Sportster tank and solo seat, could be substituted for the cumbersome saddle and big tanks of a big twin Harley. Other alternative gas tanks came from Mustang mopeds and, later, from dirt bikes. The latter were fitted with tiny tanks that became known as 'Peanut' tanks. Eventually small, specialist companies started manufacturing these items and the foundations for the huge custom parts industry of today were laid.

The fad for long forks started in an attempt to increase the ground clearance of a bobbed Harley. It was easily possible to lean a big twin over enough to ground out the primary case. One solution was to fit longer forks and there were two popular ways of doing this. The first was to find the cast springer forks off a Harley VL model. They were an inch longer and fitting these changed the bike's appearance and helped out with ground clearance. The second possibility was to find a set of war surplus experimental Harley XA springers; these too were slightly longer. Later riders started extending their own tubular springers after someone discovered that Ford car axle radius rods were in the same section as Harley–Davidson springer forks. With accurate measuring and welding it was possible to extend forks to almost any length. Customizing Harleys incorporated new parts from the factory's bikes as they became available; telescopic forks appeared on the Hydra-Glide and these soon appeared as customized bikes. The 1955–57 'straight-leg' frame rapidly became a favorite around which to build a chopper because of its clean lines. It was described as a straight-leg to differentiate it from the 1948–55 'wishbone' frame. The descriptive terms refer to the shape of the front downtubes – the straightleg is regarded by many as the first custom frame. Certainly its lines are still being emulated by frame makers more than thirty-five

Harry, of Chopper Club Wales, aboard his custom FLH (far left), while the almost spindly lines of a chopped seventies Shovelhead (left), with its long forks and modified frame, contrast with a solid looking Pro-street drag-style nineties custom (right).

years after the last one was made by Harley themselves. The Duo-Glide, a Harley with rear suspension, arrived in 1958 and custom bikes from then on were often based around swingarm frames. This was despite some feeling that a chopper should have a rigid frame. The irony is that something that appears so alternative and radical is, in fact, steeped in tradition. Frames were lengthened, raked, stretched and modified as choppers became more extreme through the sixties and seventies. In these decades modifications were frequently, but not always, to change a Harley's appearance rather than improve its handling or performance. Hunter S. Thompson provided a snapshot of a mid-sixties chopper in his seminal book, **The Hell's Angels**. He points out that outlaw bikes of that era carried only the extras required by law, such as lights and a rear view mirror (even this latter item was sometimes reduced to a minimum through the use of a dentist's mirror – apparently there was no mention of a minimum size in California highway laws). The Angels' (and other clubs) bikes used small gas tanks, no front fenders, bobbed rear fenders, skinny front wheels, upswept exhausts, tiny headlights and tall sissy bars as well as all sorts of chrome and flame painted trim. In awed tones, Thompson wrote of the chopper of the time, 'it is a beautiful, graceful machine and so nearly perfect mechanically . . .'. And so it was.
The seventies saw the Shovelhead engine in a swingarm frame become the raw material for the next generation of custom Harleys. This happened alongside trends to increasing sophistication and ostentation in the diverging styles of custom motorcycle and subsequent growth in custom parts industry, as well as a brief dalliance with Japanese bikes on the part of many builders. The current Evolution engine, introduced during the eighties, would bring builders and riders back to the Milwaukee fold in droves as well as new styles of custom Harley. These styles have been boosted further as longstanding hot rod builders and designers such as Pete Chapouris, Boyd Coddington and Thom Taylor have turned their attention to Harleys.

Above and right: Tall, skinny front wheel, no front fender or brake, springer forks, apehanger bars, jockey shift, solo seat, pillion pad, rigid frame and flames. This '42 Knucklehead is a perfect reincarnation of an early chopper. It belongs to Mark Finstad from Watertown, South Dakota, who built it over the past three years. Craig's Custom in Watertown rebuilt the engine and Randy Lauen sprayed the base coat and the flames.

Larry Pitts is a resident of New Jersey. He is seen here (far left) riding the early style chopper he built using only the correct period parts from the fifties. These include upswept fishtail pipes and a tiny, Sparto, taillight (left). Vintage style horns and jockey shifts (above) were also popular then. One of the reasons for jockey shifts was that they did away with the cumbersome linkages to a tank-mounted gearlever. This meant that it was possible to change gear more quickly while racing from the stoplight. Their removal also cleaned up the lines of the bike. Jockey shiftlevers have been adorned with everything from door knobs through dice and poolballs to pistons.

Left and right: A Panhead chopper based around the Duo-Glide style of bike – it has suspension both front and rear. The frame has been modified to accommodate the 8in. over length telescopic forks. It has belonged to Jeff Lorimer from Omaha, Nebraska, for four years. The bike features a foot clutch and hand gearchange lever, which is located behind the rider's left leg. This system is referred to as a 'jockey shift', or sometimes as a 'suicide shift', because the rider cannot put his left foot on the ground at junctions. On this bike the shifter (right) is a chromed .38 pistol.

Below: Choppers such as this Shovelhead have several inches extension built into the downtubes of the Harley FX frame; this raises the headstock sufficiently to fit extended forks but still keeps the engine and bottom frame rails level in relation to the ground. The wheels are Invader custom parts and the rear shock absorbers Smith Strutters.

Left: An FL Harley '74 chop built in the nineties. It uses the late sixties swingarm frame and engine as well as a variety of other Harley parts. The solid looking bike is a timeless combination of 21in. front wheel and 16in. rear, cut down rear fender, slightly overstock length forks, apehangers and flames. Disc brakes are a concession to modernity.

Below left and right: In the seventies, Ness and others pioneered the Bay Area Lowrider style of custom. The bikes, which were not always Harley powered, were long and low. Ness built this bike in 1975 using a '65 Sportster engine, a custom frame and springer forks of his own manufacture. It features a 15in. rear wheel and a 21in. front and a prism tank. The whole bike was adorned with wild graphics. By chance, the bike was stored in a garage in its original form for seventeen years until Bill Haar bought it and wheeled it into the sunshine again.

Left and below: Dark Star, a custom painter from Texas, built this Evo chop along traditional lines but with modern components. He used a Denver's Choppers rigid frame which is based on the old Harley straightleg design and fitted an FXR engine, an '89 transmission and a '91 FXR front end. Dark Star has been riding rigid choppers for thirty years. The seat is an old custom part re-upholstered and the taillight and sissy bar are new custom parts.

Right: In the legendary movie *Easyrider*, both the heroes ride Panheads. Peter Fonda, as Captain America, rode a chopper with a stars and stripes paint scheme. That movie, more than any other before or since, focused attention on the chopper as a symbol of freedom and has inspired many to base their bikes (as right) on Fonda's.

Above left: Although this is a contemporary custom Harley–Davidson, its influences are clearly drawn from Indian's post-war range. The Indian Chief motorcycles featured such hugely valanced fenders and enjoyed an opulent standard of fittings.

Above: Modern versions of the Bay Area Lowrider such as this neatly assembled custom are probably what the nineties will be remembered for. Billet aluminum, high tech brake parts, painted graphics and a long low look are all fashions that have come to the fore recently.

Left: Performance-styled machines such as this, which formerly belonged to Cory Ness, have always existed but, despite the fitting of a turbo and massive carburetors, its function is more for show than serious racing action.

Right: Paint schemes such as this are not exclusively reserved for custom Harleys or even motorcycles in general but can be found on jet skis and sail boards. This, from Paragon Custom Cycles, was the first Harley a nineteen-year-old painter had done.

This bike was built in the nineties to replicate a fifties-style custom Harley and uses only parts that would have been available then; the pipes, taillight and apehangers are typical. The Panhead engine was available from 1948 to 1965.

SPECIFICATION

Name
Tavern to Tavern
Owner
Larry Pitts
Builder
Owner
Location
New Jersey, USA

Engine model
H–D Panhead
Capacity
74cu. in.
Year
1964
Modifications
Fishtail exhausts

Frame model
H–D rigid
Type
Straightleg
Modifications
None
Forks
H–D Springer

Front wheel
21in. spoked
Front brake
H–D drum
Front fender
None
Rear wheel
16in. spoked
Rear brake
H–D drum
Rear fender
H–D bobbed

Handlebars
Apehangers
Gas tank
H–D Fatbob
Seat
Solo saddle

Paint
Owner
Plating
Stock

THE PROCESS OF CUSTOM BUILDING

AS CUSTOM BIKES have evolved so have the processes involved in building a custom Harley. Where once all it took was a hammer, a hacksaw, a welder and a little imagination, now it is considerably more complex but still requires imagination. In many ways the processes involved have diverged enormously; at one end of the scale is the huge and well-equipped commercial custom bike shop where the only limit to what can be built is the amount of money in a customer's pocket. At the other end of the scale altogether is the person who is modifying his or her only bike through a combination of ingenuity, catalogue and homemade parts. Often as not this person is working in a domestic garage with limited numbers of tools. Having said that, the small operator still benefits from the commercial operations as the recent growth in aftermarket parts suppliers and their ranges means that it is usually possible to buy a custom part knowing it will both fit and look good. The aftermarket industry has done the research and development for the customer. While it could be that the big custom shops don't need help with the techniques involved with building custom Harleys, the individual rider often does. Over the years magazines – such as **Easyriders** – have pointed riders and builders the right way and often led the fashions for custom bikes by featuring particularly spectacular and avant garde machines. Other publications have helped out too. In the late seventies, **Street Chopper** magazine published a series of small guides to chopper building that covered aspects such as electrics, frame and tank modifications, custom front ends and a styling guide. A truly excellent publication aimed squarely at home builders is Mike Geokan's **Custom Chopper Cookbook**: it is something of a combination of Zen and the art of motorcycle maintenance and a Clymer workshop manual! Whichever end of the scale you're looking at custom building from, it is still a combination of aluminum and steel, paint and chrome, rubber and leather and hours at the work bench, for these are the things that make a custom bike. Whether it is built in an air-conditioned factory or on the floor of a garage the same basic process must be followed. First the builder has to decide what sort of custom Harley is to be built: chopper, lowrider or drag-inspired performance bike? Mild custom or radical? Nostalgic or up to the minute? Once these questions have been answered then work can begin. The key to the whole bike is the type of frame used; a lowrider, for example,

The beginnings of a custom project (far left) – English B&I Engineering replica frames. Hours at the work bench are what ensures that bikes built by their owners, such as Denny Lueders' Shovel (left) end up looking exactly right. Nostalgic-style choppers often require traditional techniques such wheel building.

must have a long, low frame that sits close to the road while a chopper may need an early type rigid frame. Is the frame to be modified? The lowrider might want the frame stretching, as lengthening is described, to enhance its long low lines while the chopper frame might require the downtubes modifying to enable the headstock to be raised to accommodate longer than stock length forks. It could be that a frame will be purchased from a specialist frame shop. Further components for the custom have to be picked to suit similar criteria. The type of forks, tank, seat, wheels and brakes are all affected by the style of bike being constructed. Many of the current wave of high tech customs incorporate high quality aircraft-style engineering and use materials from this industry such as anodized aluminum and stainless steel. The advent of the CNC milling machine has fueled an industry dedicated to manufacturing parts, everything from wheels to handlebar grips, from billet aluminum. A more traditional Harley custom may require older parts and lead the builder to shops that stock genuine old Harley parts or pattern copies. In many ways building a traditional chopper is more like restoring a vintage ride than pure innovation.

The hours in the workshop are taken in assembling the bike to make sure that the parts both fit physically and look right. After all, the aesthetics of the finished bike are what it will be judged on and no matter how much money is spent, if it doesn't look exactly right it will always be an also ran. Those who still perceive bikers as an unwashed horde of surly misanthropes would probably be surprised at just how state of the art the technology that is used in the fabrication of custom bikes is. Both machining and welding, for example, are carried out to the highest standards as a poorly constructed custom bike soon deteriorates once it is ridden. The vibration from a V-twin engine will crack welds and bondo, as will the loads imposed by braking and cornering. All these aspects of a custom bike have to be finished before the parts go to the chromers or the paint shop.

Left: Back Off is a completely custom built Harley. It uses an Arlen Ness 2in. stretched frame, a Ness swingarm and wideglide telescopic forks. Performance Machine brakes, wire spoke wheels and numerous billet parts complete the ensemble.

Above: This performance style Harley was built by La Fores of Lakewood, CO. It is based around a Shovelhead engine and a rigid frame. The frame was stretched 2in. and lowered. Modifications were also made to fit the wide rear wheel and tire.

Below: Harley's Softail frame has rear suspension but looks like a rigid, or hardtail. Use of such a frame requires rear fender struts. In Ron Simms' Bay Area Custom Cycles workshop (see also pages 94–5) a billet strut is being tried for fit.

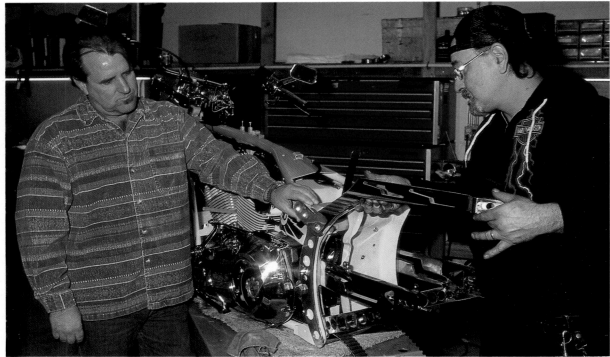

Left: The headstock of a frame must be precisely engineered to the correct angle to suit the forks. This extreme Sportster chopper has very long forks that necessitate a high headstock, evidenced by the space above the engine. The headstock must be braced to prevent vibration cracking it. The engine is also steadied by a bracket on the frame.

Above and below: The headstock of this Ness chopper (above) is braced by a combination of horizontal tube and steel gusset while the Knuckle-head chop from Texas (below) relies solely on a gusset. This style of frame is extended forwards and described as a 'gooseneck'. Like the prism tank it was popular in the seventies but turns heads in the nineties.

Above and right: Rear suspension is not uncommon on custom Harleys. The swingarm (above) mounts the rear wheel and the bottom shock absorber as standard but is a tubular item designed by Arlen Ness. Plunger rear suspension – a spring mounted axle – (right) is an antiquated design of motorcycle rear suspension. Custom builders have kept it in use, notably Amen of California with the 'Savior' frame in the seventies. This is a nineties Cobra Engineering plunger frame.

Left: Springer forks, so-called for obvious reasons, were the type of forks fitted to Harleys by the factory in the thirties and forties and so appear on many early custom bikes. These are standard length, another early feature before later extended forks became popular.

Below: In 1949 the Harley factory started using telescopic forks in a model called the Hydra-glide. This also used a Panhead engine and a rigid frame. It was a look that became popular for choppers. This bike, on Daytona Beach, is a variation on that theme. It uses extended forks and a custom frame.

Above: This chopped Sportster uses what are commonly known as girder forks. These were common on pre-war British bikes but offered advantages to the custom builder in that they could be made to any length and their slender, minimal components looked attractive, especially when chromed. Long girder forks became popular in the seventies but have largely been superseded.

Left: The high tech braking and suspension components used by the Japanese manufacturers have started a trend toward more high tech Harleys, particularly in Europe. This British owned Harley uses a complete Suzuki front end including 'upside down' forks. These are named because the lower part of the fork leg slides inside the upper. Traditionally, telescopic forks are the other way about.

Left: In the late seventies and early eighties Arlen Ness used to manufacture custom Springer forks that were more delicate than Harley's own. As recently as 1994 he used some new old stock ones on his Knucklehead powered chopper. The bike also uses a rigid frame, a taildragger rear fender and apehanger bars and certainly echoes earlier times.

Above right: Pat Kennedy from Tombstone, Arizona, is building choppers with long forks. Although some would say this is an outdated concept, Kennedy's bikes are bang up to date and perfectly engineered – with careful calculation of rake and trail angles – to ensure that they are easy to ride. The forks on this Alien machine are 30in. over stock length.

Below right: Another current custom Harley that echoes earlier times is Danny Franssen's Bobber. Franssen is from Genk in Belgium and based his bike around genuine stock length Harley Springer forks and Hydra-Glide rigid frame to give an immediate post-war appearance but used a new Harley Evolution engine and four-speed transmission.

All that these wheels have in common is that they are round and fitted with disc brakes; widths, diameters and methods of construction vary. Traditionally, Harleys have wire spoked wheels that have forty spokes. Custom builders have found a way to increase the number of spokes used (above) and can lace them up in different configurations. A minimal number of spokes are used in this American chromed steel wheel (above right) and this English made stainless steel wheel (below). Current cast alloy wheels (below right) need even less. This is a three-spoked wheel sourced from a Japanese bike. The style of wheel is chosen to suit the style of bike.

A contemporary style of wheel is that machined from a single piece of billet aluminum such as the solid wheel (above) partially hidden by a huge fender of the more visible spoked design fitted to this custom Springer (above right). Alloy combines both strength and lightness of weight, making it ideal for performance applications.

Right: The wheels for this custom Sportster were made by Performance Machine Inc. from California. They are machined out of billet aluminum and are one of the range of wheels supplied by this company who also manufacture braking components. The bike was built by Battistinis in Bournemouth, England.

Top left and above: Rear wheels and brakes are equally important; the origins of solid wheels (top left) are in drag racing. A very strong wheel was required to withstand the power of a competition engine. Three-spoke cast alloy wheels such as this (above) give a sporting appearance, even in a rigid frame, and can easily be matched to a different sized front wheel.

Left: Brake calipers such as this have become very popular in recent years. They offer excellent braking capability. Billet-6 calipers are made in England, although similar products are made in both America and Europe. The number 6 indicates that there are three pairs of hydraulic pistons and brake pads inside the caliper.

Right: The idea of modifying the existing bike rather than simply replacing everything is still current. This rigid framed (ie without rear suspension) chopper uses a stock Harley wheel, brake disc and caliper. These parts have been fitted to a custom frame with a neat variation on the flames theme.

Below: The choice of wheels and brakes is determined by the style of custom that the builder is trying to achieve. On this recent custom the current style of wheels and brakes is reflected in the choice of billet handlebar fittings, foot controls and boards and engine and gearbox parts. It is finished with a suitably modern paint job.

Left: Many custom Harleys retain the stock fatbob gas tank: it is attractive, strong and designed to fit a big twin Harley frame as well as holding several gallons of gas. The dash-mounted speedo and ignition switch enable the builder to keep the handlebars clean looking.

Below left: Another advantage of the big fatbob tank is that there is room for special paint. Flames are traditional custom paint on both choppers and street rods. There are, however, endless variations on the theme. Shapes and sizes vary quite considerably, as do colors.

Right: The airbrush paint work on this tank shows Miraculous Mutha, a lewd character who starred in **Easyriders** magazine for many years. The bike's owner, Ken Schultz from Nebraska, admitted that the guy at the window is a caricature of himself – the Moonlight Bandit.

Above: This custom tank is described as a 'Mustang tank' because it is the type originally fitted to a Mustang moped. Demand for such tanks exceeded supply so they are now manufactured especially for Harleys and available through custom parts suppliers. Both single and twin cap versions are made.

Left: Sportster tanks are a popular choice with custom builders. In the early days of chopper building they had to be obtained from the K model Sportster but replicas are now manufactured. Mounting it on the frame's top rail, as this bike, is described as 'Frisco style'.

Above: One off custom tanks are another way to go. Pat Kennedy used this faceted steel tank on his Alien machine to continue the unnatural theme throughout the bike. Its angles are reflected in most of this chopper's components, including the handlebars and air filter.

Right: Tanks, of course, do much more than just hold gas. They provide another area of the Harley that can be extensively modified. This Sportster tank, on another Pat Kennedy bike, has been fitted with a sight glass fuel gauge, ensuring it is one of a kind.

It is hard to believe that this completely rebuilt and beautifully finished custom cruise, photographed on Daytona's famous beach was once a worn out Sheriff's Patrol bike sitting in an auction yard.

SPECIFICATION

Name
FXRP Custom
Owner
Mike Tockey
Builder
Owner
Location
Fort Myers, Florida

Engine model
FXRP
Capacity
84cu. in.
Year
1987
Modifications
+.020in. Wiseco pistons
Milled heads
Andrews cam

Frame model
FXRP
Type
Swingarm
Modifications
Rake increased 4°
Swingarm stretched 3.5in.
Forks
Showa telescopic
Front wheel
18in. billet aluminum
Front brake
H–D discs and calipers
Front fender
Ness
Rear wheel
18in. billet aluminum
Rear brake
H–D disc and caliper
Rear fender
Ness

Handlebars
Ness
Gas tank
H–D FXR
Seat
Corbin Gunfighter

Paint
Jim Perno/Pat Clelland
Plating
The Chrome Factory

ENGINES

BECAUSE SO MANY of the roots of custom biking are in competition Harleys which emulate the style of early competition bikes, it is perhaps not surprising that much of the aftermarket parts industry produces parts that make Harleys go faster. Particularly in these high tech days such parts seem to be used as often on street ridden bikes as on race bikes. Many of the early tuners have left a legacy in that their hard won and homespun experience laid the foundations for the performance Harleys of today. Most people have heard of S&S Cycle Inc. and their performance parts. The company was founded by George J. Smith from Chicago in 1958. He founded it with his wife Marge as partner using the experience he gained drag racing a big twin called Tramp. And Tom Sifton, a Californian Harley dealer before World War Two, made his name tuning Harleys in order to win races around California. More than fifty years later aftermarket camshafts still bear his name and the company he founded, Sifton Motorcycle Products, still thrives. Tom Sifton passed away in 1990.

The popularization of the V-twin by both the Harley–Davidson and Indian motorcycle factories is what ensured that custom biking of today would be almost totally reliant on V-twin engines. Both factories made 45cu. in. V-twin engined bikes that were the mainstay of each company's racing efforts. The races saw crowds of partisan fans cheering on their riders which of course boosted the image of each factory's products. This brand loyalty extended across the range of bikes produced, including the larger capacity flatheads also made in both Springfield and Milwaukee. Harley–Davidson introduced their first overhead valve engine in 1936. Known as the EL model, it ensured that things would never be the same again. The EL soon became known as the Knucklehead because of the shape of the rocker cover castings. It was so revolutionary that many of the features pioneered on it are still aspects of Harley–Davidson styling today, notably the wraparound oil tank and the fatbob gas tanks. Production of the Knucklehead was interrupted by World War Two but resumed briefly after the war until the Panhead was introduced in 1948. The Panhead is so described because its rocker covers look like upturned cooking pans. The Panhead engine appeared in a rigid frame with springer forks for one year and was then upgraded to a rigid framed bike with telescopic forks and called the Hydraglide. Rear suspension and electric

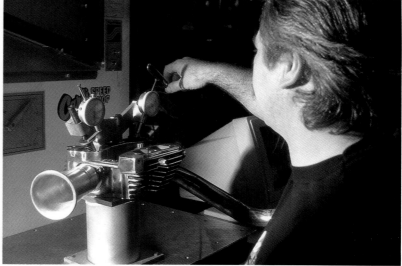

While the bike (far left) is fitted with a genuine Panhead engine, the one above is an Evolution made to look like one through the use of parts made by Xzotic Cycle Products. An altogether different approach is employed at Carl's Speed Shop (right) where they make Harley engines to go a lot faster.

starters came later, in 1958 and 1965 respectively, but it was the early Panheads that reinforced the trends established by the Knucklehead. Bikes with panniers, screens and other unnecessary accessories were referred to as 'garbage wagons' and were seen by many as merely detracting from the power of the Panhead motor because of the weight. In the mid-sixties the Shovelhead engine made its appearance and once again its nickname arose from the shape of its rocker covers which are considered to look like upturned shovels. The Shovelhead engine would stay in production throughout the seventies and early eighties, including the entire period of AMF ownership. Eventually it was superseded by the Evolution, so-named because it could trace its design roots right back to the EL model of 1936. It is the Evolution engine – which has acquired two nicknames, Blockhead and Evo – which has been responsible for the upsurge in popularity of Harley–Davidsons. It sometimes attracts disparaging remarks from the older and possibly more traditional bikers. A not uncommon T-shirt slogan reads 'See no Evo, Hear no Evo, Speak no Evo, Ride no Evo'.

There are, of course, thousands and thousands of riders who wouldn't agree with this, having experienced the advantages of greater reliability, longevity and performance of the newer engines. Having said that, it should be remembered that the nostalgic look is enormously popular to the extent that Harley–Davidson themselves have offered current bikes with fifties and earlier styling features such as two-tone paint schemes, studded saddlebags and springer forks. There are any number of aftermarket custom parts designed to make an Evolution engined bike look old including parts to disguise the engine and make it look like a Panhead or a Knucklehead. The finished appearance of engines so equipped is undoubtedly assisted by the fact that Harley–Davidson have stuck to manufacturing V-twin engined motorcycles for more than fifty years. And there is nothing quite like the spine-tingling rumble of a big V-twin.

Left: In 1936 Harley–Davidson introduced their first overhead valve V-twin engine. It was officially known as the 61E model because it displaced 61cu. in. It soon became known as the Knucklehead because of the shape of its rocker covers. In 1937, riding a machine powered by one of these engines, Joe Petrali took a motorcycle speed record off Indian on the beach at Daytona, averaging over 136mph. The legend was born.

Above: The Panhead, so named because its rocker covers looked like upturned cooking pots, superseded the Knucklehead in 1948 and remained in production until 1965. Knucklehead and Panhead engines powered the majority of early custom Harleys, notably Bobbers and Choppers. This engine may appear to be in a standard motorcycle but no Harley came from the factory sporting so much chrome.

Above: The Panhead is many people's favorite engine and is still used in freshly built custom Harleys. Fatal Attraction, built in 1992, features a monster Panhead motor that displaces 101cu. in., has dual Morris Magnetos, a dual throat carb and most of its internal components from both S&S and STD. These two companies are renowned for their performance parts. The engine was rebuilt by Williams Motors.

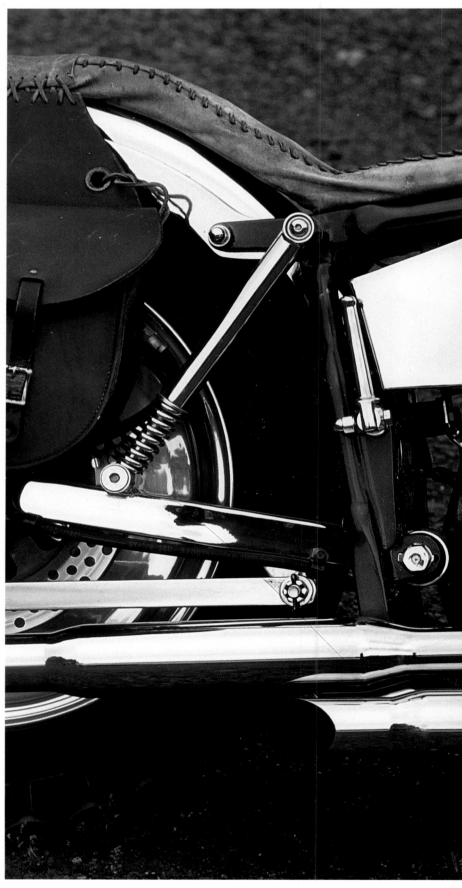

Above: The Shovelhead is so named because the rocker covers look like the backs of upturned shovels. They first appeared on Harleys from the factory in 1965. This particular Shovel is unusual in that it is assembled completely from parts available from the giant aftermarket parts company, Custom Chrome Inc. from Morgan Hill, California.

Right: This Shovelhead is from the factory; it was made in 1974 and fitted to an FX model. It now powers the chopper ridden by Ken and Jo Schultz from Mead, Nebraska. The original FX frame has been considerably modified while the engine has been equipped with an SU carb and Drag Specialties coil.

Left: The Evolution engine was introduced in the early eighties and it soon appeared in custom bikes. Custom Chrome Inc. had this orange FXR built around an Evo engine but used parts from their extensive catalogue, including the RevTech cylinder heads and carb as well as a custom exhaust and a points cover.

Below left: A less modified Evo engine, but it does have the popular S&S Teardrop airfilter cover fitted which means that one of the S&S range of performance carburetors has been installed. George Smith, one of the founders of S&S, started out drag racing and was introduced into the Motorcycle Hall of Fame in 1994.

Below right: Another popular aftermarket carburetor upgrade is the fitting of a Dellorto and manifold. Such a carb is fitted to La Bonne Vie, a Ness-inspired, British-built custom Harley. Also fitted are a Ness points cover and a custom exhaust system. Engine oil is circulated in braided steel hoses.

Left and above: Customizing is about being different and one way to achieve that is to build a performance engine with race styling for street use. This Harley (left) belonging to Trik Cycles from Florida has been fitted with a turbocharger in front of the engine. Twin Dellorto carbs on chromed manifolds supply the fuel. The Paragon Custom Pro-street style bike (above) clearly borrows its styling from the drag strip and features a 96cu. in engine with Nitrous Oxide.

Right: Technoplus, a custom shop from Aiguillon in southern France, have fitted this Harley with Mega-Four four-valve heads. There is a French connection with these parts as they are manufactured in Longueuil, Quebec, Canada, by Mega-Performance.

Left: The Harley–Davidson Sportster is also regularly used as the basis for a custom bike. Many of these are based on performance-style machines which perhaps reflects the success that the Sportster has had over the years in competitive motorcycling, especially such sports as flat track and dirt track racing. This Ironhead Sportster features exactly that style of modification, including wide flat bars and a single disc brake as well as a performance carburetor and exhaust system.

Above: Another performance
enhanced Sportster is this later
Evolution model that features a trick
twin carburetor set-up. The carbs are
fitted with race-style air filters and
have been partially painted yellow,
as has the timing cover, to coordin-
ate them with the oil and gas tanks.

Above: John Williamson of the RMD
Performance and Custom Shop in
Reading, England, built this big twin
as a street bike although it is used to
contest the UK Supertwins series of
drag racing. The engine displaces
106cu. in. and is fitted to an all-
aluminum monoshock frame. The
bike produces 110 bhp at 5800 rpm.
It is being ridden here by Dave Bartz.

Above and left: Mike Corbin devised the Warbird bodykit for Harley's FXR but this particular street bike is raced by Doug Morrow, son of Carl Morrow, who is the proprietor of Carl's Speed Shop. The 88cu. in. engine has been completely rebuilt for vastly improved performance and features a number of parts manufactured by Carl's Speed Shop. These include the magneto, camshaft, exhaust, cylinder heads and carburetor (left). Axtell pistons are also used. The transmission is five-speed although a prototype heavy duty clutch made by Barnett is installed. The frame and forks are modified FXR parts and the wheels were made by Performance Machine. The completed bike was painted in Persimmon-Tangelo pearl with flames.

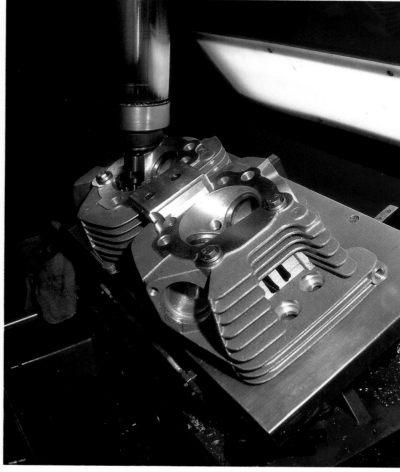

Above and right: Carl's Speed Shop is located in Santa Fe Springs, California. Carl Morrow has been in the business of making Harleys go faster since 1969 and over the years has acquired enormous expertise in engine building. He started – working from home – building engines for his own race bikes and a number of customers. His son now does the racing and the number of customers has grown immensely. The father and son team hold a number of drag racing records. His workshop now uses computers (right) in the quest for speed but still modifies engine parts, such as these cylinder heads (above) to make the engine run faster.

This Harley is typical of 1990's performance custom bikes. It features an engine with vastly increased power but the brakes and handling have been enhanced to match.

SPECIFICATION

Name
Home Brew
Owner
Steve Kenny
Builder
Owner
Location
Oxfordshire, England

Engine model
FXRS
Capacity
96cu. in.
Year
1992
Modifications
Rebuilt with increased displacement for performance by RMD Performance and Custom

Frame model
H–D FXRS
Type
Swingarm
Modifications
JMC Swingarm 3° extra rake
Forks
White Power

Front wheel
19in. Revtech
Front brake
Discs with ISR calipers
Front fender
Custom part
Rear wheel
16in. Revtech
Rear brake
Disc with ISR calipers
Rear mudguard
Owner made

Handlebars
Custom Part
Gas tank
Stock modified
Seat
Paul Nahoulakian

Paint
Owner
Plating
Bourne End Polishers

PAINT AND FINISH

THE PAINT AND VARIOUS other finishes applied to a custom motorcycle have to fulfill two functions: they have to be hardwearing to protect the motorcycle from corrosion and they have to be attractive in appearance. Paint technology has evolved considerably since the beginnings of custom biking as has the technology of other metal coat techniques such as plating. Custom painting started with brush-applied pinstripes and has evolved into an intricate art through the use of the airbrush. Like everything else the types of paintwork chosen follow fashions. In the seventies murals often showing mythical scenes of dragons were enormously popular and were sprayed on the cycle parts of motorcycles. This followed the trend of the times to adorn most motor vehicles, including cars and vans, with murals. The popularity of such paintwork has waned while beautifully detailed graphics have become the style of the nineties. There are exceptions, however, and although the style of execution has evolved the themes have remained constant. Examples are paintwork involving skulls and flames. Flames are completely timeless, traditional and they show movement as they flow around the curves of a tank or fender. Skulls are slightly more sinister, being associated with death, and seemingly reflect the flirting with danger that can be involved in riding a motorcycle with a certain bravado. The skull and crossbones symbol was long ago flown by sea-going pirates and over the years there has been an imagined affiliation with those buccaneers. A current airbrush design is achieved by spraying different colored details onto the base coat and gradually building up the finished artwork which is then coated with lacquer to give a smooth and shiny finish.

Another early influence on the development of custom painting is generally accepted to have been the nose-art painted on aeroplanes during World War Two. American pilots of both bombers and fighters often adorned the noses of their aircraft with artwork copied from or inspired by airbrush artists like George Petty and Alberto Vargas whose work appeared in magazines such as **Esquire**. The copies were done with paintbrushes and incorporated humorous names, names of girlfriends or songs. Examples are 'Jamaica' [Did ya make her?], 'Enola Gay' and 'Shoo Shoo Shoo Baby'. Many crews took this one step further and painted the backs of their jackets with the designs and the name of their ship. Many of the flyers who survived were those who

The FLH (far left) received a modern splatter paint design while this gas tank (above left) features a modern combination of two of custom biking's perennially favorite designs: skulls and flames. Gold plating such as on this wild Ness bike (above right) with twin Sportster engines was popular in the seventies.

came home from the war and bought motorcycles and so it was inevitable that nose art would appear on motorcycles and that club colors would never be quite the same again.

Steel motorcycle parts have been plated with a variety of other metals over the years: brass, nickel, cadmium, chromium, even gold. Chrome both protects steel from corrosion and is decorative. Many custom builders have considerably more of their motorcycle chrome plated than that executed at the factory. There are those who consider chrome an unnecessary extravagance – it's not uncommon to see stickers that read 'Chrome don't get ya home'. Such an attitude was possibly spawned during the late seventies when many custom bikes were so ostentatious that they bordered on the garish. It was at this time that gold plated parts were popular – if expensive. More recently, as billet aluminum parts have become popular, other types of metal coatings are seen, such as anodising. This prevents aluminum parts such as brake calipers from corroding and can be done in colors to suit a custom bike. Polishing is another way of getting a shiny finish on motorcycle parts and metals such as stainless steel and aluminum buff up to a high gloss finish. Often this is achieved by polishing the parts up with a buffing mop and, once it is refitted to the motorcycle, keeping it polished with a proprietary brand of metal polish.

Other non-metallic areas of a custom bike, such as a seat, often receive special treatment too; leather seats, for example, are often trimmed with studs and conchos, particularly on nostalgia style bikes. On more radical customs it is possible to find seats which feature colored flames that contrast with the main color of the seat.

As with so many aspects of custom bike building, the limitations on the standard of paint and finish on a particular motorcycle tend to be determined by the individual builder's imagination and ability, the technology available or the amount of money which can be spent.

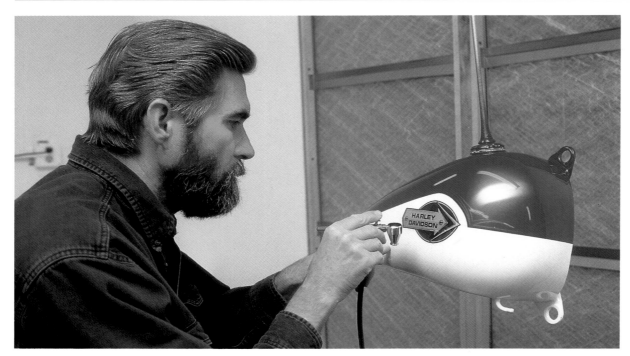

Left: Jeff McCann from Stockton, California, has been painting custom bikes for around twenty years. Here he is seen airbrushing the finishing touches of a traditional two-tone paint scheme on a gas tank. The screen behind the tank is a huge extractor fan to remove paint fumes and dust from the atmosphere.

Below: While the airbrush is one of a custom painter's most important tools because of its versatility, other older techniques are still important. McCann is painstakingly pinstriping the edges of a flame paint job on a Mustang tank in gold with a brush.

Right: The Corsa is a European built custom Sportster although it incorporates work from various American specialists, including Carl Morrow, Arlen Ness and painter Jeff McCann. It was intended to combine the elegance of Europe with the get-up-and-go of California. Jeff painted the bike in candy red and yellow. To detail the bike further he applied the goldleaf by hand to the tank, fenders and headlamp shell.

Left: Flames are traditional but on this Shovelhead chop, Arlen Ness has taken the flamed theme a step further with both flames and ghost flames. He has also incorporated flames into the points cover, air cleaner and handlebar grips. Flames are just visible stitched into the seat.

Right: Ron Simms has taken a different approach with his Evo. Not only has he used a matching selection of ball-milled billet parts, triple trees, handlebar clamp, dash panel, gas caps and aircleaner, but he has continued the flames of the tank on the speedo face.

Left: Yet another interpretation of flames on a custom Harley is seen on this street racer. The flames are painted gradually, changing color from white to purple. The tips of the flames are intertwined and on top of this are licking the orange outline of ghost flames.

Above right: The flames on Ron Rupp's custom Springer Softail (right) are still another variation on the theme. They were painted by Californian Jeff McCann before Ron rode his bike the 1500 miles to Sturgis. Rupp is a member of the Hamsters MC, a club dedicated to riding fine custom bikes.

Below right: Not the colors of flames you would perhaps expect – purple and magenta pearl. They were sprayed over the yellow paint by Damon's Motorcycle Creations on the stunning Panhead, Fatal Attraction. The flames and colors are continued on the fenders, frame and engine.

Left: Custom paintwork follows trends: flames may be a perennial favorite but murals covering whole bikes, for example, have declined in popularity since the seventies while paintwork such as this has become very popular in recent years.

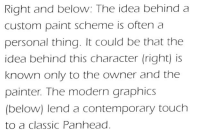

Right and below: The idea behind a custom paint scheme is often a personal thing. It could be that the idea behind this character (right) is known only to the owner and the painter. The modern graphics (below) lend a contemporary touch to a classic Panhead.

Above: Photographed at Mule Creek in Wyoming on the road to Sturgis was the Harley with this she-devil on the tank. The owner said it was his ex-wife in a way that meant he definitely wasn't joking . . .

Left: Splash paintwork such as this is another recent trend. Like flames, it shows movement and is often painted so that it appears to be flowing the length of the Harley from front to back covering the fenders, gas tank, parts of the frame and other components such as the fender struts.

Right: Skulls, and to a lesser extent, skeletons, are another favorite subject for airbrush artists to paint onto custom Harleys. This probably originates from the piratical 'Jolly Roger' flag flown by sea-going pirates of earlier times. One of the earliest and biggest outlaw motorcycle clubs – The Outlaws MC – uses a skull and crossed pistons on its colors.

Like flames though, there are endless variations on the theme. A humorous interpretation is found on the rear fender of this bike from Ron Simms' Bay Area Custom Cycles. It was painted by Horst and the 'skulls and skeletons' theme covers several other parts of the Harley, too.

Left: Starr is from Dallas, Georgia, where she runs Starr Custom Paint. She painted her Panhead yellow and then spent a further two weeks masking it up before spraying the asymmetrical black graphics. Once finished the bike won first place at the Atlanta World of Wheels Show.

Above right: Scott Entrekin left his bike with Starr to be painted. He asked for purple and left the rest to Starr. She painted the custom Harley FLH, which is unusual in that it still carries its panniers, purple but with a few neat touches of her own.

Below right: Scott's brother, James Entrekin from Dallas, Georgia, rebuilt this FLH from a basket case. He wanted it painted black in time to ride it at Daytona. Starr painted it an eyecatching blue with a modern splatter design. James liked it and agreed it turns more heads this way.

The Corsa was built in England, in a style which was intended to evoke 1950's Italian race bikes, by Battistinis, an English custom bike builder, who follow Arlen Ness's lead. Battistinis have shown that it is possible to base a stunning bike around a Sportster.

SPECIFICATION

Name
Corsa
Owner
Jeff Duval
Builder
Battistinis Custom Cycles
Location
Bournemouth, England

Engine model
H–D Sportster
Capacity
89cu. in.
Year
1992
Modifications
Rebuilt as a performance engine by Carl's Speed Shop

Frame model
Cobra Custom
Type
Plunger
Modifications
Custom built to order
Forks
Battistini Telescopic

Front wheel
21in. spoked
Front brake
Performance Machine
Front fender
Special Fabrication
Rear wheel
18in. spoked
Rear brake
Performance Machine
Rear mudguard
Special Fabrication

Handlebars
Arlen Ness
Gas tank
Battistinis
Seat
Battistinis

Paint
Jeff McCann
Plating
Battistinis

AMERICAN BUILDERS

WHILE NO BOOK COULD ever adequately cover all the custom builders in America let alone the world, such is the scale of the custom industry of the nineties, there are certain people whose names come up again and again. One such is the first of the American builders, the acknowledged King of the Custom Bike, Arlen Ness. He is a quiet, unassuming man whose wild bikes having been winning shows, turning heads and pushing the boundaries of motorcycle customizing ever wider for more than two decades.

Arlen Ness came to California as youngster from the Mid-west with his parents in the post-war years. He graduated from high school in the fifties, married at twenty and moved furniture for a living. He bought his first motorcycle, a '47 Knucklehead, in 1967 with money won at the local bowling alley. While he had already been modifying and painting cars, this was the first two-wheeler that he customized. It was taken apart and given a custom paint job. The result was that it drew a lot of comment and admiration and caused other riders to ask if Arlen would paint their bikes. The work carried out by Ness, who was still working a day job too, quickly progressed to more elaborate paint. He also started stretching tanks, modifying fenders and making up handlebars. It was a particular design of bars, ones he tagged Ramhorns, that were his first commercial success. Arlen Ness opened his first shop on a part-time basis; it was open in the evenings when he got home from his day job. He was pleased to see that somedays when he got home people were already waiting outside the shop. After customizing the Knucklehead for the second time he entered it in the Annual Oakland Roadster show. It won the ultimate accolade, the Best in Show, and made people take notice of its builder, a then unknown motorcycle customizer. He was soon able to quit his day job and turn his attention to full-time custom bike building. He still owns that first Knucklehead and, although it has been rebuilt many times over the years, it remains among his favorite bikes. Currently it is in the museum above his original shop in San Leandro in the form in which it was finished fifteen years ago. It uses unexpected components such as a Sportster transmission separated from its unit construction engine, a pair of Weber carburetors and a Magnusson Supercharger. A particular style that Ness introduced and which soon caught on, so that

Another creation close to completion on the bench in the Ness workshop (far left) contrasts with the early style chopper (above left) built far more recently than the rigid frame, apehangers, Ness springers and Knucklehead engine might imply. Housed above the workshop is this 1980 Shovelhead (above right).

numerous shops emulated and developed the style, was that of the Bay Area Lowrider. It happened in the early seventies and his bikes had long, low frames, kicked out front ends but with swept back handlebars and shortened front ends. The bikes were lean and mean, narrow and almost spidery. The lowrider style is still being developed.

Over the years he has been in business, Ness has built in excess of one hundred show-stopping bikes using turbochargers, superchargers, a twin engine configuration, Knucklehead, Panhead, Shovelhead, Evolution and Sportster engines. He has also worked on other bikes – such as one a couple of years ago in conjunction with Drag Specialties to promote their range – and supplied parts for countless numbers through the ever expanding parts side of the business. The newest color catalogue runs to more than 200 pages and features both Ness custom motorcycle products and clothing but showcases many of the parts through inclusion of bikes built in the San Leandro shop and beyond. These include bikes such as Flamin' Ape and collaborative projects such as Drag-Ness, a machine built with Drag Specialties and a number of bikes built in other countries by companies using his parts. All this of course wouldn't be possible without assistance and, as well as his employees, Arlen Ness can rely on three particular members of his family – Bev, Sherri and Cory. Bev, Ness's wife of over thirty years, works in the office as does daughter Sherri, while son Cory now runs a lot of the business and builds a neat line in bikes too. He built his first custom around a 1974 Sportster while he was still at school and it made a magazine feature in January 1981. There is a certain irony in the fact that Bev is so involved in the motorcycle business because she is one of the reasons Arlen didn't buy his first motorcycle until he was twenty-eight. Neither Ness's father nor Bev would allow him to ride a motorcycle. When Arlen turned up at home with that first Knucklehead, Bev is reported to have told him that either it went or she did. History shows that they did resolve their differences.

Left: Arlen Ness builds himself a new bike each year for the ride up to Sturgis. For 1994 he built the luxury liner that he describes as a custom bagger. It is the bike in the background of this photograph and is so-called because it carries custom panniers. Ness is standing with another bike that he built at the same time. He describes this as a hot rod because it is powered by an 89cu. in. Sputhe motor built by Jeff Border and uses a lightweight chrome molybdenum frame.

Left: This sleek motorcycle is a current version of the Bay Area Lowrider style that has existed since the seventies. The style has always verged toward long and low. Ness has long been a proponent of such motorcycles. He built this one recently using many handcrafted parts and incorporated neat touches such as the almost completely enclosed rear tire. For this reason it might be described as 'where Bay Area lowrider meets luxury liner'.

Above: The fact that Arlen Ness has, in recent years, built a selection of old style choppers has helped popularize such Harleys again. The two seen here were built by him in California and shipped to Europe to showcase his custom parts through European distributors. The yellow one – a Softail Evo – is a progression from the other – a hardtail Shovel.

Pat Kennedy

THE OWNER OF THE eponymous Pat Kennedy's Custom Motorcycles in Tombstone, Arizona, Pat Kennedy recently relocated his business there from California. Pat and partner Brook Bryant had been considering a move but were finally spurred into action when California's helmet law came into force. Pat Kennedy is a longstanding custom bike builder; he never really wanted a stock bike and built his first custom – a BSA chop – at the age of twelve. The way he saw it back then was that choppers were cool so that is what he wanted to ride. From that first BSA he has never looked back, believing that despite all the refinements in factory produced bikes there is still a place for the innovative custom builder. Pat Kennedy started building bikes at home for himself and for others who appreciated his work. One thing led to another and in 1979 he opened his first shop in Oceanside, California. He built bikes with long forks in tune with the trend and fashions of the time but, perhaps because of his early influences, stuck to building long-forked bikes although the detailing, components and craftsmanship evolved with the times. After a trip to Sweden he was impressed with the long-forked style of chops that the Swedes seemed to have made their own. Somewhat ironically, he found himself reimporting the concept of the long forked chopper to America.

The bikes that roll out of his Tombstone shop are truly bespoke. Pat, Brook and a carefully selected team concentrate on building extremely high quality custom motorcycles by limiting the shop's output to as few as six motorcycles per year. Before a bike is commissioned Pat Kennedy and the prospective owner discuss the details, such as what sort of bike the customer wants and how he wants to ride. Assuming it is all to go ahead Pat will take a number of measurements including height, weight and arm reach. From there graphic artist Jeff Cahill draws up seven scale drawings of how the finished bike might look including varying paint schemes. Jeff has been working with Kennedy for more than six years. Once the customer has seen the drawings and chosen one then work on the actual bike itself will start.

One bike built in this manner was for Bandit from **Easyriders** magazine who reportedly weighs 225lb and stands over six feet. He came to Kennedy's shop with an idea for his bike: a hardtail Evo chop with springer front end and any number of neat touches. Pat Kennedy liked the notion. The engine was rebuilt by Lee Clemens of Departure Bike Works in Richmond, Virginia, and

Pat Kennedy (far left) with two of the bikes he has built. He built this bike (above left) for his business partner and fiancée Brook Bryant. It features 20in. over stock forks and 120-spoke wheels. His own bike (above right) has a completely alien theme reflected in the angular appearance and fiendish paint.

Pat Kennedy built a frame to suit Bandit's size and to match Cahill's concept of the finished bike. The bike utilized a Sportster tank that was both narrowed and lengthened and a completely handmade rear fender. Brook Bryant laced up a pair of 80-spoke wheels an 18in. rear and 21in. front. Darrell Pinney, who paints all the bikes that Kennedy builds, sprayed the bike which was completed for Sturgis in 1992. Similarly painstaking work has been carried out on the bikes that Pat Kennedy and Brook Bryant themselves ride. Pat had an idea for a futuristic chopper with an alien theme and with his assistant Ray Neff created it around one of Kennedy's own chrome molybdenum frames and a pair of 32in. over stock forks. To give the bike an alien feel, almost everything on the machine was angled and faceted including the handlebars, frame tubes, air cleaner, gas tank and rear fender. To take that theme a step further Brook laced up 80-spoke wheels with diamond cut spokes. The final touch was the paint, applied by Darrell Pinney, which features any number of skulls and extra-terrestrial characters.

Brook Bryant's bike is dark red and silver with 20in. over forks. The curved shapes of the tank and other components are slightly more traditional but based around a similar chrome molybdenum rigid frame with a 10in. stretch and 45° rake. It is proof that with correct engineering in terms of rake, trail and seat height the rider does not have to be over six feet tall to ride a really long forked chopper. The ruby bike features glassfiber fenders and gas tank of Kennedy's manufacture. The oil tank is made from aluminum as are the forward controls and handlebars. The latter items are anodised to match the bike. Brook laced up her own 120 spoke wheels: 19in. in diameter for the front and 15in. in diameter for the rear. The brakes are made by ISR. The bike features any number of neat touches such as a one-off aircleaner. Darrell Pinney, who Brook also considers to be the best, then applied the paint in a complex scheme of skulls and graphics. The result is, as one would imagine it to be, quite outstanding.

Ron Simms

RON SIMMS BUILT HIS first bike – a custom Panhead – over a few months of 1969 and rode it around California's Bay Area. This particular Panhead was fat bobbed, lowered, fitted with a Wideglide front end and painted gloss black. The bike was different – and hot – enough to get noticed around the Bay Area. Two years later he discovered that a Harley dealer on Mission Boulevard, Hayward Harley, was moving premises so he called the realtor and signed the lease the following day. He drove down to Los Angeles for some stock and opened the place as Bay Area Custom Cycles. He didn't intend just to stock other people's parts for long though, and was intent on building bikes. Ron Simms started by building Sportster choppers – they were lowered and featured springer front ends and straight bars. Building such bikes when the fashion was for very long front ends soon ensured Ron earned a reputation for doing things differently. Ron acknowledges one of his early influences as a guy called Ron Granato who built bikes in the late sixties. As late as 1972 most custom bikes were black but Ron started using lots of color and the foundations for his reputation were laid. He is still in the same shop on Mission Boulevard today and over the course of more than two decades has seen a lot of custom-bike fashions come and go. He believes that much of the custom scene started around the Bay Area as in the sixties the styles were in the main NorCal or Frisco-style choppers; but then guys around the bay started using rigid frames with wideglide front ends, short rear fenders and Sportster tanks, high bars and foot pegs up high and of course jockey shifts. To be different, though, Simms started building bikes with understock length front ends and a correspondingly decreased rake – bikes that appeared short and fat when they were complete. Around the turn of the decade adverts for Bay Area Custom Cycles in magazines such as **Street Chopper** read 'Fat's where it's at but lean is mean' and offered frame kits and springers for Fat-Bob and Lowrider motorcycles. A particular bike built at this time by the shop was known as Gold Rush. Built for Paul Brill, it was based around a 1962 Sportster engine and used a BACC frame and springers. Also used was one of Bay Area Custom Cycles' own custom glassfiber rear fenders. Mechanically the Sportster was upgraded by the fitting of a Rajay turbo. The whole lowrider was painted white with goldleaf and approximately six ounces of gold were used to plate parts such as the

Far left and above: Ron Simms on one of his custom Harleys outside his Hayward, California, shop. The low and wide classic FL custom shown in the pair of Softails seen above, has been a trademark of Simms' for many years. Lowered frames, full fenders and wide handlebars enhance the fat look.

wheels, forks and turbo. Years ago, Simms, who has degrees in Mechanical Engineering and Architecture, saw some billet aluminum parts on a racing motorcycle. Keen to innovate, he fabricated some aluminum triple trees for his shop built bikes. It was several years later before such components became popular and more widely used.

While fabricating custom parts has always been a part of Bay Area Custom Cycles' business, as evidenced by the custom rear fenders supplied years ago, it is, alongside the custom building, an increasing part of the business now. The Bay Area Custom Cycles' catalogue lists 800 billet parts that are available off the shelf to dress up a Harley. The shop also stocks a range of quality parts from other manufacturers. A recent development is the custom frame which is the result of a joint project between Ron Simms and Ron Paugh of Paughco. It is a Softail frame but engineered so that a builder can use up to a 6in. wide rear wheelrim and a 180 rear tire but retain the factory belt drive system. Bay Area Custom Cycles has eight employees who build approximately forty-five original custom bikes per year with around twenty being worked on at any one time. Some of these are speculative builds and put on the showroom floor for sale after completion while others are built to order. They'll build whatever the customer wants. The shop does all its own work with the exception of upholstery and plating. Bay Area Custom Cycles offers service, repairs and restoration service. One thing that Ron Simms is proud of is that all his custom bikes are built for riding.

He describes his main goal as always having been to build motorcycles that not only look great but are also fully functional; otherwise he feels that it's not worth it. As proof of this, Simms' catalogue contains a number of shots of bikes he built both for himself and from customers being ridden to and from shows. Also included are old pictures of his and Carl Simms' choppers back in the early seventies. Ron rode a Panhead with apes and Carl a colorful rigid Shovel.

Bob Dron/Donnie Smith

STARTING OUT IN the custom bike world at the end of the sixties, **Bob Dron** entered a bike in the San Francisco International Motorcycle Show in 1969 and won. He started out in business in 1970 in Concord, California, and has been a central figure in the Bay Area Custom scene ever since. His first business was an outfit called American Chopper Enterprises which he ran until 1981 when he bought a Harley–Davidson dealership in Oakland. His first bike was a Triumph Thunderbird which he customized himself in the maintenance shop of his father's trucking business. Bob admits that he was influenced by guys such as George Barris who were building lead sled cars and indeed he worked on some cars himself. A lot of the bikes built by Bob Dron ended up as magazine features, such as one featured by **Street Chopper** in April 1976. The list of parts and contributing workers reads like a who's who of customizers from the seventies. It featured a Shovelhead engine in a Jammer frame with 12in. over Ness springer front end; gas and oil tanks were from Paughco. The chopper was painted by Arlen Ness and featured artwork by Horst. A particularly unusual machine he built was The Indycycle which was a Harley and sidecar with a body like an Indycar. The finished machine was track tested at Sears Point by Bob Bondurant. Another radical three-wheeler from Dron's shop was the Cycletron which had a wild design of bodywork and paint by Art Himsl. Bob fondly recalls the seventies as a decade of paisley patterns and psychedelic paint jobs.

The official Harley–Davidson dealership he runs – Oakland HD – is the largest in the world but it wasn't an altogether easy transition. He took on the franchise in 1981 and stuck with the company through the uneasy early days of their return to private management. It was, of course, worth it and trade picked up and continued to grow, so in the nineties Dron moved into new 21,000 square feet premises. In this shop there are displays of bikes and a hot rod or two as well as the expected parts department and a Motorclothes department. The latter segment of the business is run by Dron's wife, Tracey. The service department boasts an area specifically reserved for building custom bikes such as the awesome Heritage Royale.

Donnie Smith was born in Minnesota and started out as part of a team campaigning a Willys Gasser at the drag strip. One thing led to another and before long Donnie Smith was one of the brothers behind the Smith Brothers

Recently Bob Dron has been noted for building full fendered custom bikes such as the red Heritage Royale (far left) that won a major trophy at the '92 Oakland Roadster show and the purple Heritage II (above left). Donnie Smith rode his (above right) striking custom Evo to the 53rd Sturgis Rally.

and Fetrow shop in Minneapolis. The other guys were Happy Smith and Bob Fetrow. This was in the late sixties and SB&F was a respected chopper shop. It stocked many of the custom brands available then and manufactured lines of its own. In the early eighties the shop moved into larger premises and as well as stocking custom parts the shop was busy building bikes. Engine building was farmed out to Jim Ulasich who was famous for racing a Knucklehead while paint went to guys like Kevin Winter and David Bell. Fetrow and Happy Smith ran the workshop while Donnie handled the retail side of the business. In the mid-eighties the three partners moved with the times and in, view of the changing nature of the custom bike business, closed their shop. Donnie intended to take some time off then get another job at another chop shop but in the event started building bikes in a small shop attached to his home. Part way through building a customer's bike he got bitten by the bug to finish a project that he had started in the old Smith Brothers and Fetrow shop. It was a radical machine involving lots of hand-made parts but, despite this, Donnie felt that it needed some updating. One area he felt needed attention was the engine; the project had been started around a Shovelhead but in the intervening years the Evolution engine had become widely accepted. Jim Ulasich converted the Shovelhead bottom end to accept Evolution cylinder components which he drilled and tapped for a second set of spark plugs. Kevin Winter painted the bike which was widely acclaimed and ensured more customers would be seeking his skills. Among them were Drag Specialties who contacted Donnie Smith with a view to having a bike built to showcase their products. Smith built a headturning, hot pink Fat Boy which appeared on the cover of the company's 1992 catalogue. The custom styling enhanced the low fat lines of the stock Fat Boy by almost exaggerating them. The finished custom sat lower than stock and featured fuller fenders and a chainguard that followed the lines of the fender. The pink paint was detailed with scallops of a different shade.

Rick Doss/Mike and Felix La Fore

BASED IN DANVILLE, Virginia, **Rick Doss** started with customized Harley–Davidsons in 1976 when he purchased his first Harley, a 1976 Super Glide. Like so many of the talented and prolific American custom Harley builders he produces a large number of custom bikes. Custom builders may produce catalogues showing examples of their work and of their finished project bikes but, unlike motorcycle factories, they don't produce an annual catalogue of new models mainly because each new bike is one of a kind. As a result it would be hard to keep a track on the progress of the top notch builders but for the monthly output of custom Harley magazines. There is a huge variety of them worldwide now, their numbers increasing in direct proportion to the growing Harley and custom market around the globe, but undoubtedly the most famous is **Easyriders**. It is claimed to be the world's largest selling motorcycle magazine and for more than two decades has entertained, shocked and informed in its own unique style. The magazine contains a mixture of news, events coverage, pretty girls wearing nothing but a smile and of course customized Harley–Davidsons. While it has moved with the times it still relies on this successful formula. It is noticeable that certain builders appear on a not-infrequent basis: Arlen Ness, Al Reichenbach, Dave Perewitz and Bill Gardner to name but four. Yet another is Rick Doss, who once traded under the name of Rick's Custom Harlees but is now known as Rick Doss Inc. The change of name is not particularly important when it is possible to find examples of fine bikes built or worked on by Rick Doss in copies of **Easyriders** magazine that are more than ten years apart. In 1984, for example, he helped out on a custom '63 FLH; in 1986 there was the Knucklehead he built for his wife Dixie and in 1987 it was a hardtail shovel. In May 1988 a Shovelhead he had built that had won the café class at The Rat's Hole Show in Daytona made the magazine. In August of the same year another Shovelhead, this time a '76 model, appeared. In 1989 a trick Evo Softail custom appeared and so it goes on. In August 1994 a similarly trick Shovelhead complete with some of Rick's own design of parts was shown. Given the competition to get bikes featured in the magazine that is a very impressive list and it no doubt enhanced Rick Doss's reputation as a first-rate custom builder.

The giant aftermarket manufacturer Custom Chrome Inc. obviously liked what

Rick Doss (far left) built this Softail Evo custom (above left); it is one of a long line of custom Harleys built by Doss since 1976 when he first started out. The Evo Softail (above right) was built by Mike and Felix La Fore in their Lakewood shop for Hawaiian tattooist Thomas Dias.

they saw and had Rick build some of their custom project bikes using lines from their catalogue. Some people would claim that bikes built from bolt-on parts aren't true custom bikes; Rick Doss proved otherwise. Through careful selection of parts he created a stunning FXR-type custom based around a CCI five speed, rubbermount frame and a number of RevTech engine parts. A second bike he built for the company was based on a stock Harley Softail frame and featured a variety of Custom Chrome, GMA brakes and a number of Rick's own parts. It is no surprise then to find many Rick Doss Inc. parts alongside those of Ron Simms and Arlen Ness among the range distributed worldwide by Custom Chrome Inc.

While the custom bike building shop run by **Mike and Felix La Fore** is perhaps smaller and definitely younger than the others described here, it is up and coming. The brothers are based in Lakewood, Colorado, and build varying styles of bike from rigid Shovelheads that they describe as café sport (because of their low lines and bikini fairings) to Harleys that feature trick engineering. One such is a bike built for a customer, Thomas Dias, that features an incredibly trick primary cover in which the billet Derby and Inspection covers rotate when the engine is running. The Derby cover has been machined with 'directional' slots. The rest of the particular Softail is similarly trick; molded within the handmade rear fender are both the turn signals and taillight. The gas tank features an aircraft-style flush fitting alloy filler cap. The engine has been rebuilt to displace 93cu. in. and features twin-plugged heads and an S&S Super carb. High tech brake master cylinders from Performance Machine and Bill Gardner's Omaha-made GMA brake calipers are installed. Each component on the bike has been chosen either for its function or its form and then polished or painted to suit. The painted parts are finished in a lustrous black that contrasts perfectly with the alloy and chrome and the whole Harley has an air of impeccable finish and phenomenal attention to detail.

Lawayne Matthies

BORN AND RAISED in Sioux Falls, South Dakota, Lawayne Matthies saw the annual Black Hills Motor Classic take place each August in nearby Sturgis from an early age. He hasn't missed a rally in Sturgis in twenty-five years despite having relocated to Grand Prairie, Texas, in 1980. He's been building and buying, swapping and modifying bikes since he can remember. After moving to Texas he started making plans for his own aftermarket business actually to market some of the parts he had ideas about, the pivit of all those hours spent working on Harleys. The business he established is called Xzotic Cycle Products and he has taken a different route to many other custom builders. While they set out to change most of the cycle parts of the Harleys they work on but retain a stock-looking Harley engine even it is fitted with aftermarket parts, Lawayne set out to change the appearance of the engine. It would still look like a Harley engine but one considerably older than it actually was. His timing fitted in with the trend toward nostalgia and retro bikes so parts that suited this style would be popular. The Evo engine was introduced in 1984 but Lawayne didn't buy one until 1986 when he purchased an accident damaged bike from Corpus Christi. He refurbished the damaged big twin and began manufacturing retro parts to make current FL models look like much older FLs. The major parts he designed and subsequently had manufactured were a set of parts to make the heads of an Evolution look like those of a Panhead. These comprise a Panhead-type rocker cover and gasket, an adapter ring and gasket that bolts to the cylinder heads. To allow the kit to be used with later model frames the Panhead covers are available slightly shallower than Harley's originals. To increase the similarities with a Panhead he made an early style ribbed generator cam cover that retains the modern electronic ignition. He also supplies a kit that simulates the generator and distributor for further subterfuge. The parts were a success and Lawayne followed them with vintage style exhaust pipes, coil covers, battery boxes and footboards. He also turned his attention to the front end of Harleys. Following the vintage theme he design a shrouded headlamp nacelle conversion for the forks of a late model Softail.

Following a much more up to date theme in the opposite direction, Lawayne developed an electronic speedo for the tank mounted Harley dash that fits into the existing dash and features an LED display. He also designed

Lawayne Matthies runs Xzotic Cycle Products which specializes in making current model Evos look like fifties Panheads (far left). He is seen here (above left) astride the Xzotic Eye on Daytona Beach. The bike has a theme of ellipses running through it, even in Dark Star's paint on the tank (above right).

innovative headlamps that he has called the Xzotic Eye. These are typical Harley headlamps, both Bates-style and nacelle mounted, except that they are elliptical in shape rather than circular and lend a decidedly custom appearance to a Harley. Then, in time to be unveiled for Sturgis, one year he followed the success of his Panhead covers with components made to make the Evolution engine look even older. He devised a kit that recreated a Knucklehead top end on an Evolution motor. Each head is refitted with a number of castings and fittings to give the classic appearance of the Knuckleheads. When they are used in conjunction with a circular air cleaner it takes more than a second glance to verify whether or not it is a real thirties engine.

To display all his products Matthies has built bikes that incorporate them. A retro FL first came with Panhead covers and all the associated early engine parts, including the timing cover and generator/distributor assembly. The cycle parts also benefitted from the Xzotic battery box, coil cover and headlamp nacelle used in conjunction with a Corbin seat and wide handlebars. He built the Xzotic Eye, a motorcycle which not only used an elliptical headlamp but carried the theme of ellipses throughout. Elliptical taillight, footboards, turnsignals, mirrors and dash are all to be found as well as high tech parts such as R.C. Components drag race wheels. Both these bikes were painted by Dark Star, as was his third machine built to showcase the Knuckleheads. It played on Harley's advertising for the Road King which read, 'Grandpa was a Knucklehead'. Matthies built one of his custom machines that looked similar to a Road King right down to the paint scheme but actually had a 'Knucklehead' engine.

Recently Lawayne Matthies has moved his business to larger premises to allow the business to grow. Some of his parts have been used on bikes built by the likes of Pat Kennedy and are now distributed by one of the biggest American distributors as well as a major European one.

Corporate Custom

TOWARD THE END OF the sixties it became apparent that there was a market for custom parts for motorcycles and, while lots of shops made a few parts and carried out modifications, some guys were intent on bigger things. Among the first was Mil Blair who founded Jammer Cycle Products with Joe Teresi. The company produced a series of publications, **Jammer's Handbooks**, which featured technical information and a catalogue of Jammer parts and helped bikers get custom motorcycles on the road. Other companies were started back then too: Drag Specialties based in Minneapolis started out making Maltese Cross taillights and mirrors. Tom Rudd founded the company in a small retail shop and saw the operation grow massively during the seventies. In 1971 Custom Chrome Inc. also started in a small store; there were others, too, including Paughco and Gary Bang. The market continued to grow and other companies joined the line up, including Chrome Specialties Inc. from Texas and Zodiac International BV from Holland, both of which were founded in 1984. Chrome Specialties was founded by two brothers, John and Greg Kuelbs, after they sold their official Harley–Davidson dealership in Texas. They moved to Arlington, and established their aftermarket business. Recently they acquired the famous Jammer brand and launched a new line of parts under the Motor Factory name. Zodiac International BV, as the European arm of an American company, started in a small Amsterdam warehouse with only three staff and 2000 square feet of warehouse. In 1990 the company moved into a 50,000 square feet facility in Mijdrecht, Holland.

What all these companies do is produce a selection of parts for Harley–Davidsons. The parts range from being service items such as filters and brake pads to replacement standard parts for repairs and restoration and, of course, a huge selection of custom parts. The major companies produce huge catalogues – often in excess of six hundred pages – that show their range, list part numbers and often cross refer them with Harley's own part numbers. The beauty of this is that it is possible for a customer to choose the components he or she requires, find the part number for the item to fit his or her own bike and order it through the local dealer who stocks that brand. The aftermarket parts companies have highly organized distribution networks and many local bike shops carry one or more of the brands. Another aspect

This FXR (far left) was built by Rick Doss for Custom Chrome Inc. using parts from their catalogue. John Reed is an expatriate Englishman who works for CCI. He built this Evo (above left) for the Fiftieth Anniversary of Sturgis. This custom Shovelhead (above right) was built by the company from products out of their catalogue.

of these big companies is that they distribute specialist products from smaller or more specialist manufacturers.

The major companies produce such a comprehensive range of parts for Harley–Davidsons that it is possible to build a complete and rideable motorcycle from the products in the catalogue. What each company does is build project bikes to showcase its own components; these take various forms. In some cases the company has teamed up with a particular custom builder to produce an extra special custom bike. Arlen Ness collaborated with Drag Specialties on at least one bike, while Rick Doss worked with Custom Chrome Inc. on several projects, for example. Another type of corporate custom are bikes such as the Custom Chrome Inc. and Chrome Specialties machines which are built solely from that company's products. Recently Chrome Specialties have even prepared a 'shopping list' of the parts required, to help a prospective builder order sufficient compatible parts to build a custom bike – there are 266 part numbers on it. While these companies and others such as Nempco and V-Twin Manufacturing are the largest concerns in the corporate custom business there is a new wave of manufacturers growing with the market. Arlen Ness and Ron Simms are long-established custom builders but are increasingly producing product ranges for sale through other motorcycle shops and both produce color catalogues of their ranges. Ness produces a huge range of billet aluminum parts and items such as frames and swingarms. Ron Simms produces his own range of billet parts and has collaborated with Ron Paugh of Paughco on some frames. Pro-One are another of the new wave manufacturers of frames and billet parts. A spin-off of the wide availability of sufficient custom parts to build a motorcycle is that companies are building complete bikes for sale to customers. Two such companies are California-based Illusion and Big Dog Motorcycles Inc. from Kansas. This is in addition to the enterprises seeking to relaunch other famous American marques such as Indian and Excelsior.

The style of apehangers and flames has never gone out of fashion for choppers. This is a nineties version of the old theme and uses many high tech parts alongside the traditional styling. CNC-machined components and disc brakes are just some of the modern parts.

SPECIFICATION

Name
Flamin' Ape
Owner
Arlen Ness
Builder
Owner
Location
San Leandro, California

Engine model
H–D Shovelhead
Capacity
74cu. in.
Year
1980
Modifications
Ness covers and aircleaner

Frame model
H–D Rigid
Type
Wishbone
Modifications
None
Forks
Paughco Springers
Front wheel
21in. spoked
Front brake
Disc and Performance Machine caliper
Front fender
None
Rear wheel
18in. spoked
Rear brake
Disc and Performance Machine caliper
Rear fender
Ness Taildragger

Handlebars
Ness Apehangers
Gas tank
Arlen Ness
Seat
Danny Gray

Paint
Arlen Ness
Plating
High Luster

EUROPEAN INFLUENCES

EUROPE HAS ALWAYS had a motorcycle culture; some of the world's most famous makes came from factories in Great Britain, Italy and Germany. As in America, the enthusiast scene was focused around competitive events and in particular road racing. Events such as the Isle of Man TT Races annually attracted thousands of riders to the island to see the racers battling it out on the twisty roads of the mountain circuit. Riders emulated the style of race bikes with race-style seats, tanks and handlebars and congregated around coffee bars – the so called café racers. In 1969 the film **Easyrider** was shown at cinemas across Europe. It was a breath of fresh air that heralded the winds of change, coming as it did in the decade of flower power and a changing world order. If choppers were good enough for Peter Fonda and Dennis Hopper as Captain America and Billy respectively, then they were cool for Europe too. The problem was that, with one exception – the 45 – in Europe Harley–Davidsons were not plentiful. Because of the numbers of ex-army WL models left behind by the the various armies it was possible to ride a chopped Harley. In France, Brigitte Bardot had just such a chopper and she recorded a song about it. In London John Wallace and Ray Leon had a shop building choppers from the then plentiful WL models. If a Harley engine wasn't available, the alternative was to chop one of the plethora of British bikes. The sudden enthusiasm for choppers prompted disapproval from the established and serious sort of motorcyclist. One journalist commented that an Englishman riding a chopper was as unnatural as a Mexican wearing a kilt. Many motorcyclists didn't agree and chopper building continued unabated.

Times moved on and Harleys became more widely available in many European countries. A trickle of custom parts were imported from America but things really took off in the early eighties when two things happened. Ton Pels, a Dutchman, opened Zodiac International BV near Amsterdam which specialized in custom parts from around the world. Harley–Davidson introduced the Evolution engine and sold them in Europe. With the raw material more widely available it was inevitable that the whole custom bike scene would become more Harley–Davidson orientated. That is exactly what happened and in Holland, France, Britain, Sweden, Norway and Germany are to be found huge numbers of Harley riders. The popularity of custom Harleys has spread beyond these countries of course: Italy, Spain and the

Airbrush Willy (far left) is a Belgian who earns his living by custom painting. Completely contrasting styles of show standard custom Harley: a luxury liner (left) and a pair of traditional rigid choppers (right). What they do have in common though is that they were built in Europe, in France and Scotland respectively.

former Eastern Bloc countries are seeing increasing numbers of Harleys on their roads.

The different types of riding conditions experienced in Europe, in terms of weather conditions, more frenetic traffic and, in some cases, stricter legislation, have led to various different types of modifications being made to Harley–Davidsons. For example, the more frequent salting of roads to keep snow and ice at bay means that many custom parts are made from corrosion-resistant stainless steel. The prevailing traffic conditions and the existence of such things as roundabouts has encouraged the uprating of braking equipment. The strictest legislation concerning modifications to motorcycles in Europe is found in Germany where all custom parts have to be approved by a certain government department. This hasn't stopped German customizers but has had a bearing on what they manufacture.

One style of custom Harley that seems almost exclusive to Europe is a combination of a Harley engine and frame but with the front end and wheels from a Japanese sports bike. The idea behind this is that the builder ends up with what can be described as the best of both worlds. He has a Harley–Davidson with a series of performance modifications that enhance both the appearance and abilities of his motorcycle. The complete front end of a Japanese bike that would be utilized features twin discs and high quality calipers as well as cast alloy wheels that can be painted to complement the remainder of the bike. One of the reasons for this type of modification is simply that the parts are more plentiful and less expensive than corresponding performance Harley parts. This situation is changing though as the popularity of Harleys continues to increase in Europe.

With this increasing popularity is coming a much larger market and one that will support a specialist aftermarket for Harleys. As a result, it is now possible to find custom shops, engine builders and tuners, bike restorers and unofficial Harley shops in most European countries.

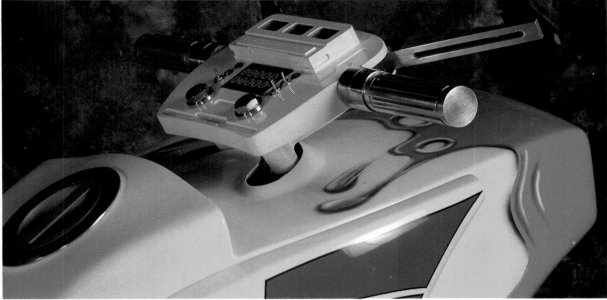

Custom bike building is all about building something different. Hans Boekhoue from Bourne, Holland, has gone one step further and built something totally unique around a Shovelhead engine and transmission. The bodywork is completely hand made from steel sheet and incorporates both oil and gas tanks. The speedo (above) is electronic and has a digital display. The handlebars turn the front wheel through the bodywork that carries the headlamp and flows into the downtubes of the frame. Boekhoue did all the work himself, including the paintwork, with the sole exception of the seat. This is designed to allow room for the travel of the rear suspension. The bike runs and Boekhoue regularly rides it to Harley rallies and shows in Europe.

Left: Richard La Plante, the American martial arts novelist who lives in London, England, had this 1989 FXSTS customized by Battistinis, the British custom shop. The engine was rebuilt by Alan Fisher at Ultimate Performance in London to an increased displacement of 95cu. in.

Below: Englishman and long-standing custom Harley rider Andy Peters built this motorcycle from Harley parts and specially fabricated sheet metal. He emulated the long, low 'luxury-liner' style of custom that has become popular in the USA. Both the induction and exhaust systems are particularly intricate.

Right: Nicolas Chavin from Paris, France, built this spectacular Shovelhead lowrider as a tribute to the blues musician Stevie Ray Vaughan. He did all the work himself including making the frame in which to fit the 1980 engine and transmission. The forks and front wheel are from a Suzuki while the rear wheel is an alloy car item fitted with a specially machined hub. Chavin also sprayed the murals and graphics onto the bike which subsequently won many custom show trophies.

Above and right: In Europe the Swedish are famous for building radical choppers with extremely long front ends. Seen here are two examples of such bikes. Above is Boi Andersson's Panhead. He is from Satrabrunn and his bike club is housed in an old silver mine. Andersson did all of the custom work himself including converting the frame to a hardtail in his spare time. The green chopper (right) belongs to Peter Koij from Falun in Sweden. He built it in six months. It is based around a 96cu. in. Evo engine and Sputhe transmission. The rigid frame has been fitted with a Sportster tank and Tolle forks that are 24in. over stock. Careful attention to rake and trail means that such bikes are rideable; indeed, Koij and Andersson ride their bikes at least 1500 kliks each summer on a two week run.

Above: Bill from Bristol, England, built this chopped Shovelhead along traditional lines. It features a rigid frame, apehangers, solo seat, fishtail exhaust pipes and a Sparto taillight as well as a traditional scallop paint job. The valanced rear fender probably owes more to Indian's styling than Harley's. Attention to detail shows in the fact that the plug leads, air filter and Derby covers and even the valve caps on the wheels have been color coordinated yellow to match the fenders and gas tank.

The high tech approach to custom Harley building that is popular in Europe is clearly demonstrated by this Evo, built by Technoplus, a French custom shop from Aiguillon in southwest France. While this bike is based around a Softail frame, much of the remainder was specifically made by Technoplus with the aid of a CNC-milling machine. The wheels, fork legs, brake calipers, hand and foot controls were all made in France. The combined seat and tank unit, known as the Monobody, which brings to mind both traditional fatbob tanks and modern sportsbikes, was also manufactured by Technoplus.

Left and below: Rick James from Cleethorpes, England, is a relative newcomer to the custom bike building scene but has been turning out show standard Harleys for the last couple of years. This 1986 FXST (below) was completely rebuilt in his workshop for a customer, Sue Barnes, from Guernsey. Many of the modifications are very subtle and are aimed at cleaning up the overall appearance of the Softail. Japanese wheels and forks add a high tech look to the bike which is further enhanced by the use of a Ness fairing and rear fender. As much as possible of the Harley was painted black by Rick's brother, Paul.

Right: The combination of a Harley engine and frame with Japanese wheels, forks and brakes is a popular one in Europe. This lime green Evo, built by The Legend Bike Shop from Belgium, is another example of such a bike. It uses Kawasaki wheels, brakes and fork legs although the latter items have been fitted to wideglide yokes. The contemporary paint scheme was sprayed by Airbrush Willy who is in his second year as a professional.

Below right: Dave King, a member of the Outlaws MC from the English Midlands, constructed another variation around an Evolution engine in a Santee custom rigid frame. The forks are the 'upside down' style ones and were made by Suzuki for a GSX-R. Using the complete front end gave him twin discs and four pot calipers on a three-spoke cast alloy wheel.

The advent of the CNC milling machine has certainly revolutionized the art of custom bike building around the globe. This lowrider from France is a good example; it is the product of a specialist custom shop based in southwest France called Technoplus.

SPECIFICATION

Name
Technoplus Lowrider
Owner
Technoplus
Builder(s)
Michel Galmiche/Claude Babot
Location
Aiguillon, France

Engine model
H–D Evolution
Capacity
80cu. in.
Year
Unknown
Modifications
STD cases
Mega-four heads
S&S carb

Frame model
Custom Rigid
Type
Chopper Guys
Modifications
None
Forks
Technoplus
Front wheel
17in. billet aluminum
Front brake
Technoplus caliper and disc
Front fender
Technoplus
Rear wheel
17in. billet aluminum
Rear brake
Technoplus caliper and disc
Rear fender
Monobody

Handlebars
Technoplus billet
Gas tank
Monobody
Seat
custom

Paint
Stevy, Lyon, France
Plating
Technoplus

UNSUNG HEROES

BIKERS ON HARLEYS haven't always been as popular as they seem to be today when every actor, actress or singer who wants to be someone is slipping on a black leather jacket and throwing a leg over a Harley. For a long time, riders of motorcycles were treated as second-class citizens for a variety of reasons. Maybe it was the fashion for long hair and beards; maybe it was the wild reputation bikers had; maybe it was the bad publicity generated by occasional violent incidents; or maybe it was just the worry that your daughter would ride into the sunset behind some 'scooter trash on a chopper'. The bad publicity was a two-way thing – movies like **The Wild One** vastly exaggerated an incident that happened at the AMA sanctioned races at Hollister, California, in 1947 that was reported in **Life** magazine and a few years later there were a succession of what have become known as biker-exploitation movies. Club wars and general mayhem at some of the long established events such as Laconia, Sturgis and Daytona didn't help and attracted a heavy police presence at these events and threats of their being ended. Despite all this the custom bike scene thrived thanks in no small way to magazines including **Easyriders**, **Choppers** and **Iron Horse**, a network of bike shops and clubs who continued to put on events and shows and of course those who lived for the thrill of being 'in the wind'. They truly were the unsung heroes of custom biking.

Another reason why things didn't look so bright for those aboard Harleys was that the market share of motorcycle sales held by the Milwaukee factory was shrinking annually. During the seventies Harley–Davidson was under the control of American Machine & Foundry. Quality control wasn't what it might have been and the last American motorcycle manufacturer was facing devastating competition from the Japanese makers (A similar situation with regard to competition had existed earlier from the British manufacturers but Harley had brought out the Sportster to compete.) The Japanese were producing cheaper, faster and more reliable motorcycles, the first Japanese win at the Daytona 200 was in 1970 and with one exception it has been that way ever since. Honda really stuck the knife in with their advertising slogan, 'You meet the nicest people on a Honda', the clear implication being, of course, that you don't on a Harley. Despite this, a lot of bikers stuck with Harley–Davidson, tolerating unreliable machines and discrimination. The

Dark Star (far left) riding his rigid framed Evo chopper built from parts. (Above left) Bill Bultz's Shovelhead chop required the electric starter cutting off the primary case to make room for the jockey shift linkage. (Above right) Steve Mastine on the 1984 Shovelhead that he bought new that year.

custom scene continued although a surprisingly large percentage of the custom shops made, or stocked, parts for Japanese bikes.

Somewhere it all began to turn around. It is hard to define why, when or exactly where it started. The movie **Mask**, starring Cher and based on a true story, showed a more compassionate, caring side of bikers, The Harley–Davidson Company official campaign on behalf of the Muscular Dystrophy Association, Harley's return to private ownership and better quality control, the introduction of the Evolution engine all helped to improve the public's perception of the Harley rider. Even the formation of the Vietnam Veterans' Motorcycle Club was seen by many as a statement that bikers were proud Americans who did their duty, too. On a similar but slightly different note, the Hells Angels MC ran a campaign whose slogan was 'Hells Angels are Americans too' after some of their members faced discriminatory legal action through the courts. Bikers around the world formed pressure groups to protect their rights to ride: ABATE – A Brotherhood Against Totalitarian Enactments, in America; MAG – Motorcycle Action Group, in England; and FEM – Federation of European Motorcyclists, in Europe.

The other type of unsung hero is the biker who doesn't have a huge and well-equipped workshop and has only one bike. He spends the grocery money to get the custom bike on the road. He works on it during evenings and weekends with the limited facilities of a domestic garage and the assistance of his riding buddies. Despite all this, or possibly because of it, he wheels out a show standard chopper. Not for him the glitz of Hollywood and its weekend riders but nights at the local biker bar, local toy runs and helmet protests, scouring the swap meets for parts, shows and parties and runs with his riding buddies with perhaps occasional rides to the annual events in Sturgis, Daytona or Laconia. At these he's the guy with bedroll strapped on the forks and a tent on the cissy bar rather than the one with a Harley in a pickup bed.

Left and top right: Robby Tomlinson from Jacksonville, Florida, astride the Panhead he built up himself after just buying the engine. The Panhead engine was rebuilt by Michael's Cycle of Mayport Beach who increased the displacement to 86cu. in. The frame forks and rear fender (right) are new custom items from Paughco but are styled after forties' and fifties' Harley parts, giving the whole bike the look of a classic chopper. Up to date touches include the Jaybrake calipers and disc brakes and the vibrant paint.

Right: Similarly vibrant paint adorns Jeff Lorimer's chop. The resident of Omaha, Nebraska, seen here partially rebuilds his bike – which is another variation on the chopped Panhead theme – each winter in preparation for the next year's riding. It uses a swingarm frame and a dresser strutless rear fender.

Right: The Hog Farm is typical of many independent, unauthorized Harley shops that exist around the world carrying out performance, custom and restoration work. The Hog Farm from New York has been run by Ruth Grottanelli and her husband Grott since 1969. It takes its name from the old slang term for a Harley – a Hog. Custom Harleys were referred to as chopped hogs. The Hog Farm built this big twin for Ruth using mostly custom and aftermarket parts. It is a 98cu. in. Shovelhead in an Arlen Ness frame and swingarm. This and a wideglide front end have been fitted with solid cast S&S wheels. A custom rear fender and seat sit behind the fatbob gas tank which features a dash with a digital Cyberdyne speedo. Other custom parts include the drag bars, mirror, grips, tail lights and license plate frame.

Above and right: Shane Ferguson from Minnesota wheelying his café race Sportster. He used parts and technology from high tech sports and race bikes to build this custom Harley himself. It features carbon-Kevlar panels, a race-type fairing, a British JMC alloy swingarm, Works Performance shock absorbers, 43mm Showa forks, cast alloy wheels, a D&D Muffler and (right) a performance engine rebuilt by Carl's Speed Shop from Santa Fe Springs, California. The engine was increased in capacity from 883cc to 1200 and now features S&S pistons, ported heads, a hot cam, S&S carbs and Screamin' Eagle coil and ignition module.

Left and below left: Clive Maye from Chester, England, riding his custom Panhead. The Harley is based around a genuine and rare '55–'57 straightleg Harley frame. Its straight lines give a neat and uncluttered appearance to the finished bike. A custom flat rear fender is supported on specially fabricated struts that flow into the tail light. At the front are a pair of early '80s FX custom wideglide forks that allow mounting of brake calipers and a 21in. front wheel.

Right and below: Steve Mastine riding his 1984 Shovelhead chop at Daytona. He has owned it since it was new and describes it as 'just a good running bike'. It has been rebuilt by Trik Cycles from Florida where Steve works, using a lot of custom parts including CCI fishtail exhausts, Trik oil cooler, Ness pushrod covers, a digital oil pressure gauge and a Corbin seat.

Above: Custom painter, Dark Star, at Sturgis on the rigid Harley–Davidson Evolution chopper that he built from parts then painted in a traditional style of flames.

Below and right: From Wahoo, Nebraska, Bill Bultz and his chopped '75 Shovelhead (right) – it has been like this since 1982. The downtubes of the frame have been lengthened to raise the headstock while it has been lowered at the rear. This means that the rider sits in the classic disdainful 'chopper' pose: arms straight, feet forward (below).

Above and left: Typical of many of the unsung heroes of custom biking are Ken and Jo Schultz from Mead, Nebraska. They have owned this Shovelhead since they bought it new as a stock 1974 FX and have been riding it and modifying it ever since. They've also been riding with the same crowd they met at a Helmet Law Protest in 1974 in Lincoln, Nebraska. Owning a bike for more than two decades means that they were riding a Harley long before it became fashionable. They also stuck by the brand through the troubled years of AMF ownership.

Right: Neilson Miller from Newcastle, England, riding his custom Softail. He rebuilt the Harley from a fire damaged wreck using a combination of genuine Harley and custom aftermarket parts. The forks, frame and rear fender are original while the gas tank, bars, mirrors and forward controls are custom items. The heavy front forks fitted with a minimal front fender and drag-style bars echoes the early 'bobber' idea of cutting down heavy Harleys to make them go faster.

Below: Neilson chose parts to enhance the triangular shape of the Softail frame. The bars and risers flow into the dash. The lines of the dash and tank flow into the seat which is contoured to follow the line of the rear fender out of which curves the Sparto taillight. The bike was photographed in the amusement arcade known as Spanish City and made famous by rock band Dire Straits.

At a glance, this Harley (left) could be mistaken for a completely nostalgic ride – a new old chopper. However, underneath the flamed paint, the apehangers and upswept fishtail pipes it is remarkably modern.

SPECIFICATION

Name
Outlaw Bike
Owner
Flint
Builder
Owner
Location
Coventry, England

Engine model
Evolution
Capacity
80cu. in.
Year
Unknown
Modifications
Mikuni carb

Frame model
Modified HD
Type
Softail
Modifications
Welded on hardtail
Forks
ZXR 'upside-downies'
Front wheel
ZXR cast alloy
Front brake
Kawasaki ZXR
Front fender
Kawasaki ZXR
Rear wheel
ZXR cast alloy
Rear brake
Kawasaki ZXR
Rear fender
Flat custom

Handlebars
Apehangers
Gas tank
King sportster
Seat
Solo seat and P-pad

Paint
Jay, Nuneaton, England
Plating
Custom Chrome, Nuneaton, England

RIDDEN NOT HIDDEN

A SHOWROOM stock motorcycle might be just a means of transportation but a custom bike is always something more. Whether it is daring to be different, simply the rider showing off, built to attract the girls or simply give its owner the satisfaction of riding a handbuilt motorcycle, it is always going to be more than a bike for getting from A to B. It is the sort of bike that will get from A to B but probably by a far more scenic backroad.

Custom Harleys represent different things to different people too; for some a bike is a toy to be ridden on a Sunday but to others it is almost the sole reason for living – 'I only ride Harleys on days that end in Y'. For some it is an easy thing to acquire, a bespoke bike bought with the wave of a credit card; for others a custom Harley is the result of hours of hard work, scrimping, saving and spending the grocery money on bike parts. Each way has its rewards. Whether the custom is for cruising Main Street in Daytona, for the annual pilgrimage to the Black Hills, or for parking outside the Club Wannabe, the characters who ride custom Harleys are as diverse as the colors on the bikes they ride. The hard-riding One Percenter is likely to have a different outlook on life to the weekend riding office worker.

A rider's outlook will affect what he or she rides; the newcomers and show-offs often want to ride a bike that is as ostentatious as possible. A veteran of years on the road is more likely to be riding a classy custom that shows its heritage through a careful choice of minimal but classic parts. Those who want to win trophies at custom shows such as The Rat's Hole Show in Daytona or The Oakland Roadster Show will be viewing the concept of custom bike building from an altogether different angle, while the guy who wants to cruise the bars looking for pretty girls is going to make sure that his is a motorcycle built for two. And so it goes on.

Other much more mundane factors, such as weather and geographical location, influence what type of custom Harley a rider is likely to be found on. Bikes without front fenders look as cool as anything until it rains. Then they become a nightmare to ride as a spray of cold, gritty water hits the rider right between the eyes! There are different fashions around the world, too: East and West Coast styles in the USA, a distinct European style and yet another style in Australia where long front ends are in the minority because of the distances that have to be ridden on poor roads. Once all these factors have

English Outlaws, Dave and Flint, on the urban streets of Coventry (far left) contrast with Taz (above left) on the rural roads of Scotland and Paragon Custom Cycles' pro-street bike in Sturgis, South Dakota (above right), but they are all custom Harleys and all being ridden.

been taken into account, often subconciously, and a bike has been built either up from a bare frame or by modifying an already extant machine, it's time to go riding. There are rides for every mood whether it be the lone rider wandering on quiet roads or a pack of Harleys coming on like a thousand-bomber raid. It might be a charity run to help some less fortunate group or it could be that the rider is heading for the mayhem of a big party. It could be that the destination is a protest run to remind (none too subtly) the politicians that bikers are voters; it might just be a run to the mountains.
The rumble of a V-twin, the clunk from the transmission as a gear is selected, the buzz of anticipation as the clutch is let out.
Get your motor runnin' and head out on the highway. Other makes and models of motorcycle may come and go but Harleys simply go on for ever. Occasionally they may be hamstrung by the men who write silly little laws about the position of turn signals or that 'objects in the rearview mirror may appear closer than they are' but, riding down the road, with the sun glinting off the chrome and listening to the backbeat from the pipes, suddenly none of that matters. There are those, particularly among the paternalistic road safety lobby, who see Harley–Davidsons, indeed motorcycles as a whole, as iron dinosaurs and wish they were extinct. Unfortunately for them motorcycles, unlike the dinosaurs, are continually evolving and it is often the custom bike builders who point the way that the evolution will take. Recently Harleys, like all other motor vehicles, had to be manufactured suitable to run on unleaded gas, due to increasingly stringent emissions regulations. The latest heinous crime a motorcycle rider can commit is to make too much noise. It is thought that under the draconian proposals for quieter motorcycles it will be impossible to market an air-cooled machine. Worldwide, many manufacturers already produce liquid-cooled bikes, and Harley–Davidson have been experimenting with a liquid-cooled racer, the VR1000, which might just be the future.

Left: The combination of components is critical so that the finished custom looks exactly right. This is particularly important with the long forks and high handlebars of a classic chopper. Scottish bikers Charlie and Logie have both achieved the archetypal appearance despite using different combinations of parts.

Above: Ken Schultz has also engineered his Harley to create the classic chopper look. The lines of the frame have been enhanced through judicious lengthening of the downtubes while the angle and length of forks mean that the handlebars fall comfortably within reach, allowing the rider that studied air of casualness.

Below: More café-racer in styling is Felix La Fore's rigid Shovelhead but its shape still allows an upright and feet forward riding position through the use of pullback bars which are mostly concealed behind the tinted perspex of the fairing windshield. The triangular shape of the rigid frame remains deliberately uncluttered.

Left and below: Women ride custom Harley–Davidsons too; Jill Stanley (left) regularly rides this heavily modified 1987 Lowrider in the company of partner, Dave Bell. Seen leaving the Hamsters MC picnic in Spearfish, South Dakota, is this lady (below) aboard a beautiful flamed custom Softail. The Hamsters MC are a club dedicated to riding spectacular custom bikes and include Arlen Ness among their members.

Right: This Harley has been modified but still retains many factory parts, including the frame. Although a Softail, it has rear suspension and was designed to look like a triangular early rigid frame. The forks too have a vintage appearance but are fitted to current models. Harley build what are often described as 'factory customs'.

Below: The Sportster chop seen at the Red River Run in New Mexico definitely isn't a factory custom. The frame tubes have been heavily modified to get the high headstock and accommodate the long custom forks as well as giving the upright riding position. The spoked wheels, Mustang gas tank, seat, small cissy bar and flat rear fender are also from a custom parts supplier.

Right: Stefan from Denmark riding his traditional-style Panhead chopper. It is essentially a Hydraglide in that it has telescopic forks and a rigid frame but the apehangers, jockey shift gearchange, Mustang tank and high cissy bar confirm it as a bona fide chopper from the old school. Cissy bars are so-named for passengers who worry about falling off backwards.

Left and below: Two custom Harleys from different eras: a sharp Ironhead Sportster at the Red River Run (left) and a more contemporary customized FLSTC (below) that belongs to Todd Tumminello. From Michigan, Tumminello bought it as a stock second-hand bike and reworked it to suit his requirements. It is a combination of old style FL and new style paint and parts.

Left and below: Bill Bultz riding his chopped Shovelhead at Sturgis. The absence of a helmet law in South Dakota is just one of the event's attractions. Also taking advantage of this in the August sunshine are the staff and friends of La Fore's Motorcycle Shop (below) who had traveled to the Black Hills from Lakewood, Colorado. They are seen here riding through Deadwood toward Sturgis. During the week-long rally and races all the towns for miles around Sturgis itself are filled with bikers who come to see such attractions as Mt Rushmore.

Right: This bike may at first glance appear to be a stock Harley from the fifties but it is typical of a nostalgia-type custom bike. It is a current model Evolution Harley–Davidson dressed up with numerous aftermarket custom parts to look like a fifties bike. Parts added include the exhaust pipes, seat, saddlebags and, of course, the whitewall tires.